Co-curricular Activities:

A Pathway to Careers

Managing Editor-Career Publications: Andrew Morkes
Project Editor: Maureen Glasoe
Cover Design: Sam Concialdi
Interior Design: Ted Glasoe
Proofreader: Anne Paterson
Indexer: Sandi Schroeder

Co-curricular Activities: A Pathway to Careers

Copyright © 2001 by Ferguson Publishing Company
200 W. Jackson Blvd., 7th Floor, Chicago, Illinois 60606
Web: http://www.fergpubco.com

Library of Congress Cataloging-in-Publication Data
Co-curricular activities: a pathway to careers
p. cm.
Includes index.
ISBN 0-89434-304-1
1. Student activities—United States. 2. Career education—United States.
I. Ferguson Publishing Company.

LB3605 .C66 2000
373.18—dc21
00-030898

Printed in the United States of America
X-9

TABLE OF CONTENTS

Chapter 11

Theater and Drama 227

Resources 255

Index 257

Outlook Note

The information in the Outlook section of each article has been obtained from the US Bureau of Labor Statistics and is supplemented by information taken from professional associations. Job growth terms follow those used in the Occupational Outlook Handbook: *growth described as "much faster than the average" means an increase of 36 percent or more; growth described as "faster than the average" means an increase of 21 to 35 percent; growth described as "about as fast as the average" means an increase of 10 to 20 percent; growth described as "little change or more slowly than the average" means an increase of 0 to 9 percent; "decline" means a decrease of 1 percent or more.*

Co-curricular Activities: A Pathway to Careers

"Extracurricular activities are important to a student's overall growth and maturity. The activities expose students to a broad array of new issues and challenges, thus enriching their experience. We look very favorably on a student who brings a rich palette of life experience into our classrooms."

— Margaret Drugovich, Vice President of Admission and Financial Aid, Ohio Wesleyan University, Delaware, Ohio

✦ ABOUT THIS BOOK

"What do you want to be when you grow up?"

You probably heard this question countless times as a young child. Chances are, you named a job related to your interests and hobbies. If you liked animals, you decided you'd be a veterinarian. If you enjoyed entertaining people, you dreamed of becoming an actor or singer.

Just because you are older now, and thinking more seriously about college and careers, doesn't mean you have to neglect those early dreams.

Take the case of the famous painter, Georgia O'Keeffe. It was reported in *The Christian Science Monitor* that when she was 12 years old, she told a friend she was going to be an artist. What if she hadn't followed her ambition? The world would never have known the beautiful flowers and desert scenes that she created.

Despite what you might think, it is possible to choose a career that relates to your personal interests and talents. In fact, choosing a job you can be truly passionate about is the best road to career fulfillment and success.

This book will show you how you can relate your co-curricular activities and interests to your career choices. Each chapter is on a particular club or activity and lists careers that correspond with it. The entry for each career will give you an overview of the job, the employment outlook for the near future, the earnings you can expect, the education and training required for that job, and ways to explore the field outside the classroom.

Check out the careers listed under your favorite pursuits, and learn about the potential of extracurricular activities you may have never considered.

In the next section of this introduction, you will learn how important co-curricular activities are in the college admission process and academic success, as well as in your profession.

Throughout the book you will find the testimonials of college admissions counselors, reinforcing the importance of outside-the-classroom activities.

THE POWER OF CO-CURRICULAR ACTIVITIES

Co-curricular activities aren't just fun—they are valuable to your future. Belonging to a club, participating in student government, or competing on a sports team is a way for you to explore your interests and enjoy your time in school. But these endeavors also expand your potential in other important ways. They:

+ build leadership skills,
+ help you to better communicate with others,
+ teach you how to work as part of a team,
+ boost your self-confidence and self-esteem, and
+ sharpen your organizational and problem-solving skills.

These qualities will be increasingly important as you move through life, whether you are applying to colleges or seeking a job.

WANTED: WELL-ROUNDED STUDENTS

It is often acknowledged that colleges are looking for more than just academic success in their prospective students. But we wanted to find out exactly how co-curricular activities ranked with college admissions counselors. So we conducted a survey.

When asked how important extracurricular activities were in their evaluation of a student for admission into their school, only 17 percent of college admissions counselors said they didn't consider them to be important at all. Five percent thought they were extremely important; 29 percent, very important; 31 percent, average; and 18 percent, somewhat important.

"Extracurricular activities play a pivotal role," says Daniel Walls, dean of admission at Emory University in Atlanta, Georgia. "What students do when they are not in class is an important question on the application. With 5,000 undergraduates, we need students to be involved and participating in our campus life programs."

Here's how the survey respondents rated various co-curricular pursuits, on average, in order of importance:

1 Student government
2 Academic clubs (including science and language)
3 Athletics
4 Music
5 Yearbook/school newspaper
6 Special interest (e.g., chess, photography)
7 Community service
8 Theater/art

The respondents also acknowledged the influence of these activities on academic performance.

"Extracurricular activities show a well-rounded student who will be successful at the university level, both academically and socially," says Amy Jensen, director of Enrollment Marketing at Biola University in La Mirada, California.

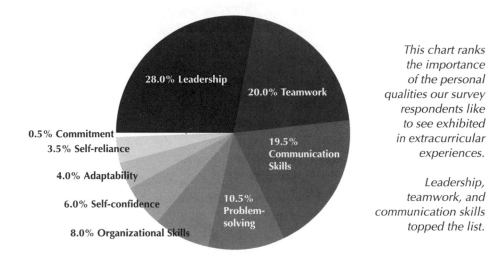

This chart ranks the importance of the personal qualities our survey respondents like to see exhibited in extracurricular experiences.

Leadership, teamwork, and communication skills topped the list.

Study after study shows that students who are involved in extracurricular activities perform better in the classroom. They tend to have higher GPAs, higher test scores, a lower risk for dropping out of school, and a greater chance of attending college.

There are several reasons for this. The first is that active students know how to better manage their time. Because they have full schedules, they know how to be productive.

Second, the pursuit of an extracurricular activity often complements classroom work. For example, performing in a play in drama club gives students a better understanding and appreciation of the plays they are assigned to read in English class. Members of the debate team are likely to give stronger oral presentations.

Finally, activities like playing in chess tournaments and serving on a student council build confidence and social skills. Self-assured, expressive students tend to be higher academic achievers.

So, besides being a ticket into the college of your dreams, your co-curricular involvement will help you succeed once you're there. It will also make you more marketable after you graduate.

◆ "ME INCORPORATED": THE WORLD OF WORK TODAY

Today's job market is vastly different than it was even a generation ago. With the growing influence of technology, everything is less static: companies tend to be less focused on the long-term, and people change jobs more frequently. This means that workers have to be more innovative and adaptable.

This trend has been called "Me Incorporated"—an environment in which you must constantly market yourself, whether you are actively looking for a job or already employed. It is becoming increasingly important that workers continue to develop their skills, pursue additional education, and make themselves the best job candidates they can possibly be.

As a high school student, you can get a head start on this process by working to develop the qualities that will make you attractive to prospective employers. Just what are employers looking for? Many of the characteristics you can develop through your co-curricular pursuits.

For example, employers want to know their employees are going to show up on time and get their work done. If you've worked on a school newspaper, you know all about scheduling and deadlines. Employers want their staff to perform well as a team, supporting one another and communicating clearly to achieve their goals. If you are on a sports team or in an orchestra or band, you know what teamwork means. Initiative, perseverance, commitment, dependability, honesty, cooperation, friendliness—all of these are qualities employers look for in their candidates.

Whether directly or indirectly, the skills and habits you are developing outside the classroom will serve you well in the world of work. So keep on doing what you love to do. This book can help you make a career out of it!

CHAPTER 1

Athletics

"A student involved in extracurricular activities [now] most likely will continue at the college level; and as an institution we would like our students to give back to the college community whether that be through volunteer service, participation in clubs and organizations, or through athletic programs."

– Megan Ryan, Assistant Director of Admissions,
Wells College, Aurora, New York

✦ INTRODUCTION

"Play ball!" Almost everyone in our society can relate to this evocative phrase signaling the start of a baseball game. America's pastime brings together people from all walks of life—and so do many other sports, from football to figure skating.

Careers in sports are not just for the athletically inclined; they encompass a wide range of professional possibilities. Many people besides athletes are needed to stage a sporting event: coaches, team statisticians, announcers, grounds keepers, and many more.

After you're finished with this chapter, you may decide that athletics is the field of your dreams.

AEROBICS INSTRUCTORS AND FITNESS TRAINERS

OVERVIEW

Aerobics instructors and *fitness trainers* guide, motivate, and teach proper exercise techniques to people interested in staying fit.

Aerobics instructors choreograph and teach aerobics classes of varying types. Classes are geared toward people who are in good health as well as to specialized populations, including the elderly and those with specific health problems, such as heart disease, that affect their ability to exercise. Aerobics classes are generally organized into three levels: low-impact, moderate, and high-intensity. Most often set to music, the classes usually involve an exercise portion and a stretching portion.

Fitness trainers create customized conditioning programs for individual clients, ranging from the amateur to the professional. Fitness trainers often work with people in their own homes or offices. They motivate their clients to follow exercise programs and monitor their progress. When injuries occur, they may work with a physical therapist to help with an athlete's rehabilitation.

EARNINGS

Aerobics instructors are usually paid by the class and generally start out at about $10 per class. Experienced instructors can earn up to $60 per class. Health club directors usually earn about $30,000 per year.

Fitness trainers earn between $15,000 and $35,000 per year, depending on geographic location and years of experience. Although a sports season may only last a few months, athletes train year-round to stay in shape, and they need trainers to guide them. Many personal trainers are paid on a client-by-client basis. Contracts are drawn up and payment is agreed upon before the training starts. Some trainers get paid according to the results they get.

◆ OUTLOOK

Because of the country's ever-expanding interest in health and fitness, the US Department of Labor predicts that the job outlook for aerobics instructors should remain strong through the year 2008. As the population ages, more opportunities will arise to work with the elderly in retirement homes. Large companies and corporations are also interested in keeping insurance costs down by hiring aerobics instructors to hold classes for their employees.

Fitness trainers are also in strong demand, especially at the high school level. Some states even require high schools to have a fitness trainer on staff. In-home fitness trainers will remain in high demand to accommodate the needs of today's busy professionals.

✦ TRAINING

Aerobics instructors and fitness trainers need at least a high school diploma. Courses in physical education, biology, and anatomy are recommended. Although it isn't always necessary, a college degree will make you more marketable.

Fitness trainers are usually required to have a bachelor's degree from an accredited athletic training program or a related program such as physical education or health. These programs require extensive internships that can involve up to 1,800 hours of hands-on experience. Essential college-level courses include anatomy, biomechanics, chemistry, first aid, health, kinesiology, nutrition, physics, physiology, and psychology.

Certification is not required in most states, but most clients and fitness companies expect fitness trainers and aerobics instructors to have credentials.

Continuing education courses and a high level of physical fitness are typically required of professionals in this field.

✦ EXPLORING

Visiting a health club, park district, or YMCA aerobics class will provide an opportunity to observe the work of fitness trainers and aerobics instructors. If possible, enroll in an aerobics class or train with a fitness trainer to experience firsthand what their jobs entail.

A part-time or summer job in a gym or fitness facility would also expose you to the field and provide training on the use and safety features of the equipment. Another possibility is to volunteer in a senior center where aerobics classes are offered.

Aerobics instructor workshops are often offered at YMCAs and other facilities to help prospective instructors gain experience. Unpaid apprenticeships are a good way for future instructors to obtain supervised experience before teaching classes on their own. Opportunities for student fitness trainers are sometimes available in schools that have fitness trainers on staff.

✦ RESOURCES

American College of Sports Medicine
PO Box 1440
Indianapolis, IN 46206-1440
Tel: 317-637-9200
Web: http://www.acsm.org/

American Council on Exercise
5820 Oberlin Drive, Suite 102
San Diego, CA 92121-3787
Tel: 619-535-8227
Web: http://www.acefitness.org

National Athletic Trainers Association
2952 Stemmons Freeway
Dallas, TX 75247-6196
Tel: 214-637-6282
Web: http://www.nata.org

GROUNDS MANAGERS AND GROUNDS KEEPERS

◆ OVERVIEW

Grounds managers and *grounds keepers* within the sports industry work to maintain the condition of playing fields of all types and the land surrounding the facilities. Much of their work involves keeping grass or artificial turf in top condition for the athletes who play on it. Grass must be regularly mowed, fertilized, aerated, and sprayed for weeds, pests, and other infestations that might affect the field's appearance and condition. Artificial turf must be vacuumed and disinfected after a sporting event so that bacteria won't grow. Periodically, the cushioning pad beneath the artificial turf must be replaced. Caring for playing fields also includes painting the appropriate boundaries, markers, and team names and logos on the turf.

Grounds managers and their crews also maintain the shrubs, plants, and flowers on the grounds of a football stadium, baseball park, or other sports arena. They are responsible for planting, pruning, fertilizing, edging, and all other aspects of keeping the landscape healthy and attractive. Some grounds-keeping crews are employed year round and others are hired seasonally.

Besides the "green" side of the job, grounds managers oversee finances, materials, equipment, and staff.

◆ EARNINGS

Grounds managers tend to be salaried employees who earn between $25,000 and $55,000 annually, depending on their education, training, and experience. By comparison, the hourly wages for grounds keepers are much lower. Most grounds keepers can expect to make between $10,000 and $13,000 a year.

◆ OUTLOOK

Candidates for grounds management and grounds-keeping positions should expect to find a large number of job openings in the future. A high turnover rate, especially among the lower-paying grounds-keeping occupations, means stronger employment opportunities.

Professional sports and the athletes who play them generate billions of dollars. Thus, the appearance and condition of a stadium or playing field is extremely important to the team and the community that supports it. Grounds managers and their crews are a vital part of maintaining a sports team's image.

TRAINING

If you are interested in becoming a grounds manager you should aim for a BS in grounds management, horticulture, agronomy, or a related field. For a grounds-management job, most employers require a minimum of four years of experience, at least two in a supervisory position. Also helpful is a knowledge of budgeting, management, and cost-accounting procedures; public relations and communication skills; pesticide application certification; related equipment and tools; and trends and developments in the field. Courses in business management and personnel management are helpful, though not required.

There are no minimum educational requirements for entry-level jobs in grounds keeping. Many grounds keepers do not have a high school diploma, although some positions require it. Some states also require grounds keepers to pass an examination on the proper application of chemicals.

EXPLORING

Grounds-keeping positions are excellent entry-level jobs for high school students aiming for a career in grounds management. Since most grounds-keeping positions are seasonal, students can work part time, after school, and on weekends during the year and full-time during the summer. Interested students should start by contacting municipal park districts, lawn care companies, nurseries, botanical gardens, and professional landscapers.

◆ RESOURCES

American Society for Horticultural Sciences
600 Cameron Street
Alexandria, VA 22314-2562
Tel: 703-836-4606
Web: http://www.ashs.org/

Associated Landscape Contractors of America
150 Elden Street, Suite 270
Herndon, VA 20170
Tel: 703-736-9666
Web: http://www.alca.org/

Professional Grounds Management Society
120 Cockeysville Road, Suite 104
Hunt Valley, MD 21030
Tel: 800-609-7467
Web: http://www.pgms.org/

PROFESSIONAL ATHLETES

✦ OVERVIEW

Unlike amateur athletes who play or compete for titles or trophies only, *professional athletes* and professional athletic teams compete against one another to win titles, championships, and series and are paid salaries, prize money, and/or bonuses for their work.

The athletic performances of teams are usually based on a cumulative score; the winning team compiles the highest score, as in football, basketball, and soccer. The athletic performances of those in individual sports are evaluated according to the nature and rules of each specific sport. For example, the winner of a track race is whoever crosses the finish line first.

In a team sport, each member specializes in a specific area. During practices, the team members focus on their role, whether it is defensive, offensive, or both. For example, a baseball pitcher spends some time running bases and batting, but the majority of his time is spent practicing pitching.

Most professional athletes train rigorously all year, varying the type and duration of their workouts to develop strength, cardiovascular ability, flexibility, endurance, speed, and quickness, as well as to focus on technique and control. Athletes often watch videotapes or films of their practices and competitions to see where they can improve their performance.

Professional teams train for most of the year, but they usually have an off-season. Following an off-season, there is usually a training period leading up the start of a season.

✦ EARNINGS

Top-level professional athletes today earn millions of dollars a year. Top players and athletes can earn as much or more in endorsements and advertising, usually for sports-related products and services but also for products or services unrelated to their sport. But for every multi-million dollar athlete, there are hundreds of professional athletes who earn much less—as little as $40,000 a year. How much financial success an athlete has is often tied not just to athletic skill, but also to the athlete's personality, character, and professional conduct.

✦ OUTLOOK

The job outlook for professional athletes varies depending on the sport, its popularity, and the number of positions open with professional teams. On the whole, the outlook for the field of professional sports is healthy, but the number of jobs will not increase dramatically. Sports that experience a rise in popularity will offer opportunities for higher salaries, prize money, and commercial endorsements.

◆ TRAINING

There are no formal educational requirements for a career in athletics, although certain training and professional opportunities are available only to those enrolled in four-year colleges and universities. Collegiate-level competition allows athletes to hone their skills, and it exposes them to professional scouts. Athletes who compete in individual sports also have the chance to compete in national or international competitions.

A college education arms you with a valuable degree that you can use if you cannot earn a living as a professional athlete or after your playing days are over.

Diligence, perseverance, hard work, ambition, and excellent physical fitness are all essential qualities for a professional athlete.

EXPLORING

Students interested in pursuing a career in professional sports should start playing that sport as often and as early as possible. Most junior high and high schools have well-established programs in the sports that have professional teams.

If a team sport does not exist in your school, petition your school board to establish it as a school sport. Organize other students into a club team, scheduling practices and unofficial games. Contact the corresponding professional association for tips on gaining recognition.

To determine if you really want to commit to pursuing a professional career in your sport, talk to coaches, trainers, and athletes who are currently pursuing a professional career. You can also contact professional organizations and associations for information on how to best prepare for a career in their sport.

RESOURCES

Amateur Athletic Union
c/o The Walt Disney World Resort
PO Box 10000
Lake Buena Vista, FL 32830-1000
Tel: 407-934-7200
Web: http://www.aausports.org/

American Alliance for Health, Physical Education, Recreation, and Dance
1900 Association Drive
Reston, VA 20191
Tel: 703-476-3400
Web: http://www.aahperd.org/

SPORTS AGENTS

OVERVIEW

Sports agents act as representatives for professional athletes in many different types of negotiations, providing advice and representation concerning contracts, endorsement and advertisement deals, public appearances, and financial investments and taxes. They may represent only one athlete or many, depending on the sport, the size of their agency, and the demands of the client or clients they represent. Agents usually represent their clients for the duration of their careers and often find work for athletes once their athletic careers are over.

Networking and tending to details are a large part of a sports agent's everyday routine. In between reviewing contracts and financial arrangements, he or she might be on the phone with an advertiser, scheduling lunch with a sports scout, or renting an apartment for an athlete for spring training.

EARNINGS

Agent commissions at top management firms run anywhere from 5 to 10 percent of the player's earnings and up to 25 percent for endorsements the agency negotiates on behalf of the athlete. Thus, sports agents can earn phenomenal amounts of money by representing a single star athlete: If the athlete earns $50 million a year or more in salary and endorsements, his or her agent would make approximately $2.5 million a year on a 5-percent commission. But the average agent makes far less. The average yearly salary for an agent just starting out ranges from $20,000 to $25,000. As the agent acquires more athletes or the status of his or her athletes increases, the agent's salary might go up to $35,000 to $40,000 per year. The high end for the typical agent is approximately $40,000 to $60,000 a year.

According to one insider, the sky's the limit; if an agent is extremely ambitious and the agent's contacts within the sports world are fruitful, he or she can earn over a million dollars a year.

OUTLOOK

The outlook in this field in general looks strong. The sports industry is thriving and there is nothing to suggest that the public's interest in it will dwindle. In fact, as cable television brings greater choices to viewers, it is possible that less-publicized sports will gain in popularity through increased exposure, thus breathing life and revenues into those sports and creating new demand.

✦ TRAINING

No educational requirements exist for sports agents, but it is increasingly difficult to enter the field without at least a bachelor's degree in business administration, marketing, or sports management. Many who eventually become agents also go on to pursue a graduate degree in law or business, two areas which increase but don't guarantee a sports agent's chances at success. Courses in contract law and economics can be particularly helpful in the negotiation process.

Contacts and exposure to athletes are the unofficial requirements for sports agents. Simply put, without knowing or having access to athletes, it is next to impossible to represent them. Personal traits necessary for success include an outgoing personality, persistence, top-notch communication skills, and savvy politicking skills.

✦ EXPLORING

Because the intense competition in this field makes it hard even to get intern positions and entry-level jobs, insiders recommend starting as early as possible and taking any job that gives you exposure to athletes. High school students can shag balls at tennis tournaments, work as a golf caddy, or apply for coveted ball boy/girl and bat boy/girl positions with Major League baseball teams.

College internships are probably the most valuable introduction to the field, especially because many of the top management firms that hire agents don't accept younger applicants. An internship will allow you a close look at the process and the nature of the work so that you can judge if it suits you.

✦ RESOURCE

International Management Group

IMG Center, Suite 100
1360 East 9th Street
Cleveland, OH 44114
Tel: 216-522-1200

SPORTS BROADCASTERS AND ANNOUNCERS

✦ OVERVIEW

Sports broadcasters work for radio and television stations, selecting, writing, and delivering current sports news for the sports segment of news broadcasts or for specific sports events, channels, or shows. They may provide pre- or postgame coverage of sports events, including interviews with coaches and athletes, as well as play-by-play coverage during the game or event.

Sports announcers are the official voices of the teams they represent. At home games, it is the sports announcer who makes pregame announcements, introduces the players in the starting lineups, and keeps the spectators in the stadium or arena abreast of the details of the game by announcing fouls, substitutions, goals, and other developments.

EARNINGS

Salaries in sportscasting vary depending on the medium (radio or television), the market (large or small, commercial or public), and whether the sportscaster is a former athlete or recognized sports celebrity, as opposed to a newcomer trying to carve out a niche.

According to the *Occupational Outlook Handbook (OOH),* the average salaries of television sportscasters range from $22,000 at the smallest stations to $129,000 at the largest. For all stations, the median salary is $49,000. Sportscasting jobs in radio tend to pay less than those in television. Radio announcers earn an average salary of $31,251 according to the *OOH,* with the low range at $23,000 and the high at $39,291.

Salaries for recognized sports personalities or celebrities can be as high as $2 million a year.

OUTLOOK

Competition for jobs in sportscasting will continue to be fierce, with the better-paying, larger-market jobs going to experienced sportscasters who have proven they can keep ratings high. Sportscasters who can easily substitute for other on-camera newscasters or anchors may be more employable.

The projected outlook is one of average growth, as not that many new radio and television stations are expected to enter the market. Most of the job openings will come as sportscasters retire, relocate, or enter other professions. In general, employment in this field is not affected by economic recessions or declines; in the event of cutbacks, the on-camera sports broadcasters and announcers are the last to go.

 TRAINING

Television sportscasters who deliver the news in sports usually have bachelor's degrees in communications or journalism, although personality, charisma, and overall on-camera appearance is so important for ratings that station executives often pay closer attention to the audition tapes they receive from prospective sportscasters than to educational background or resumes. It isn't as crucial for sportscasters who work in radio to have the physical appearance that a television sportscaster has.

Whether working for radio or television, sports announcers and broadcasters must have an outgoing personality, excellent verbal and interviewing skills including the ability to ad-lib, and a solid command of sports in general as well as in-depth knowledge of the particular sport they are working with.

 EXPLORING

High school and college students have many opportunities to investigate this career, but the most obvious way is to participate in a sport. By learning a sport inside and out, you can gain valuable insight into the plays and techniques that you'd be describing as a sportscaster. Firsthand experience and a love of a sport makes it easier to remember interesting trivia related to that sport as well.

If you do not have the skill or desire to play a particular sport, you can volunteer to help out with the team by shagging balls, running drills, or keeping statistics.

An excellent way to develop the necessary communication skills is to take a journalism course, join your school's speech or debate team, or volunteer for your school's radio station or a local radio or cable television station.

Finally, many aspiring sportscasters hone their skills on their own while watching their favorite sporting events by turning down the sound on their televisions and tape-recording their own play-by-play commentary.

RESOURCES
Broadcast Education Association
1771 N Street, NW
Washington, DC 20036-2891
Tel: 202-429-5354
Web: http://www.beaweb.org

Federal Communications Commission
1919 M Street, NW
Washington, DC 20554
Tel: 202-632-7000
Web: http://www.fcc.gov

National Association of Broadcasters
1771 N Street, NW
Washington, DC 20036-2891
Tel: 202-429-5300
Web: http://www.nab.org

Radio-Television News Directors Association
1000 Connecticut Avenue, NW, Suite 615
Washington, DC 20036-5302
Tel: 202-659-6510
Web: http://www.rtnda.org

SPORTS EQUIPMENT MANAGERS

◆ OVERVIEW

Sports equipment managers are responsible for maintaining, ordering, and inventorying athletic equipment and apparel. They work for high school, collegiate, and professional teams. Their duties vary according to the sport they are in and the size of their team. They deal with everything from sharpening hockey skates to doing the team's laundry.

Equipment managers order all of the equipment needed for teams or schools. They also fit equipment and uniforms for each player. Properly fitted equipment is critical in minimizing injury and maximizing comfort. Other duties include budgeting, purchasing, facility scheduling, and keeping up to date on current trends and products available. Equipment managers also supervise staff members ranging from paid personnel to unpaid student volunteers.

◆ EARNINGS

The equipment manager at one US university cited 1998 salary ranges of $20,000 to $60,000 for head equipment manager positions and $15,000 to $40,000 for assistants. Equipment managers' salaries are naturally higher if they work for a professional team than for a high school.

◆ OUTLOOK

The field of sports equipment management is rapidly changing and growing. With the increase in women's sports teams, the demand for qualified women's equipment managers is particularly high. The addition of computerized inventory programs, and the big-business atmosphere of athletics in general, is motivating equipment managers to broaden their range of knowledge in many new areas.

◆ TRAINING

To become a professional equipment manager, the Athletic Equipment Managers Association suggests one of the following paths: 1) high school/GED degree and five years of paid, nonstudent employment in athletic equipment management; 2) four-year college degree and two years paid, nonstudent employment in athletic equipment management; or 3) four-year college degree and 1,800 hours as a student equipment manager. Business and computer classes are also recommended.

◆ EXPLORING

Serving as the equipment manager of one of your high school athletic teams or clubs will give you a great introduction to work in this field.

◆ RESOURCES

Athletic Equipment Managers Association
PO Box 2093
Ann Arbor, MI 48106-2093
Tel: 734-741-9447
Web: http://www.wisc.edu/ath/aema

National Operating Committee on Standards for Athletic Equipment
PO Box 12290
Overland Park, KS 66282-2290
Tel: 913-888-1340
Web: http://www.nocsae.org

SPORTS EXECUTIVES

OVERVIEW

Sports executives—including *team presidents, CEOs,* and *general managers*—manage professional, collegiate, and minor league athletic teams. They are responsible for the teams' finances, as well as overseeing the other departments within the organization, such as marketing, public relations, accounting, ticket sales, advertising, sponsorship, and community relations. Sports executives handle the trading, hiring, and firing of personnel; supervision of scouting and negotiation of player contracts; and overseeing daily business activities. Sports executives also work on establishing long-term contacts and support within the communities where the teams play.

 ## EARNINGS

General managers, team presidents, and other sports executives earn salaries ranging from $20,000 to $50,000 per year in the minor leagues to more than $1 million in the majors.

OUTLOOK

Although there are more sports executive positions available due to league expansion and the creation of new leagues, such as the Women's National Basketball Association, there still remain only a finite number of sports executive jobs. The competition for these positions—particularly at the top level—is fierce. It is projected that this field will experience little change or grow more slowly than the average in the near future.

 ## TRAINING

At least a bachelor's degree is required to become a sports executive. Even though this is a sports-related position, presidents and general managers are expected to have the same backgrounds as corporate executives. Most have master's degrees in sports administration, and some have MBAs.

Excellent communication and public speaking skills are a must for sports executives. They must be able to make firm decisions while also being diplomatic.

EXPLORING

One way to explore this field is to volunteer to chart statistics or manage equipment for a sports team at your school. Talk to the general manager of your local minor league baseball club and try to arrange a part-time job with the team during the summer. When you are in college, try to get an internship within the athletic department.

◆ RESOURCES

CareerSearch, Inc.
PO Box 328
Fairfax, VA 22030
Web: http://www.careersearchinc.com

Sports Administration Specialization Coordinator
Department of Physical Education, Exercise, and Sport Science
Woollen Gymnasium, CB#8605
The University of North Carolina
Chapel Hill, NC 27599-8605
Tel: 919-962-3226
Web: http://www.unc.edu

SPORTS FACILITY MANAGERS

✦ OVERVIEW

Sports facility managers, also called *stadium* or *arena managers* or *stadium operations executives,* are responsible for the day-to-day operations involved in running a sports facility. They are involved in facility planning, including the buying, selling, or leasing of facilities; facility redesign and construction; supervision of grounds keepers and custodial crews; and development and coordination of the facility's annual operating calendar. The sports facility manager also handles the negotiations, contracts, and agreements with industry agents, suppliers, and vendors.

✦ EARNINGS

Earnings for sports facility managers vary considerably, depending upon experience, education and certification level, and the type of facility. According to an industry profile survey conducted by the International Association of Assembly Managers, the salaries of assistant- or associate-level managers ranged from $31,282 to $59,904 per year, while the salaries of general managers ranged from $46,447 to $75,801 per year. The salaries of sports facility managers fall roughly in the same range.

✦ OUTLOOK

In general, the future for facilities managers is much brighter than it is for those in other administrative services. This relatively young field is growing quickly and, especially in the private sector, is not as vulnerable to cost-cutting pressures or government cutbacks. The demand for jobs in sports administration is great, and the newer field of sports facility management is quickly catching up.

✦ TRAINING

A bachelor's degree is usually required to enter the field of sports facility management. Courses in business, mathematics, and computer science are helpful. A master's degree in sports administration or sports facility management is increasingly required of managers.

Certification in facility management is not mandatory, but it is becoming a distinguishing credential among managers of the largest, most profitable venues.

◆ EXPLORING

If you aren't actively involved with a sport as a participant, you can volunteer to assist a high school team. Any and all experience helps, beginning with organizing and managing equipment to working as a team statistician. Part-time or summer jobs as ushers, vendors, ball boys, and ball girls not only offer first-hand experience for students, but they also provide contacts and opportunities.

College students interested in sports facility management can often find internships through placement centers in undergraduate or graduate programs in business administration and facility management. Professional organizations within the field also sponsor opportunities to learn on the job.

◆ RESOURCES

International Association of Assembly Managers
4425 West Airport Freeway, Suite 590
Irving, TX 75062-5835
Tel: 972-255-8020
Web: http://www.iaam.org/

International Facility Management Association
1 East Greenway Plaza, Suite 1100
Houston, TX 77046-0194
Tel: 713-623-4362
Web: http://www.ifma.org/

Stadium Managers Association
19 Mantua Road
Mt. Royal, NJ 08061
Tel: 609-423-7222
Web: http://stadianet.vml.com/

SPORTS INSTRUCTORS AND COACHES

✦ OVERVIEW

Sports instructors demonstrate and explain the skills and rules of particular sports, like golf or tennis, to individuals or groups. They help beginners learn basic stances, grips, movements, and techniques of a game. Sports instructors also help experienced athletes to sharpen their skills.

Coaches work with a team or individuals, teaching them the skills associated with a particular sport. A coach motivates, prepares his or her team for competition, and gives instruction and inspiration during competition.

All instructors and coaches are teachers. They must be highly knowledgeable about rules and strategies for their respective sports, and be able to effectively convey the correct techniques and procedures to their students or players. Motivation is another key element in sports instruction.

Many coaches and instructors also have administrative responsibilities, such as recruiting new players.

✦ EARNINGS

Sports instructors who teach group classes for beginners through park districts or at city recreation centers can expect to earn around $6 per hour. Instructors at summer camps generally earn between $1,000 and $2,500, plus room and board, for a summer session. Full-time fitness instructors at gyms or health clubs can expect to earn between $13,000 and $28,000 per year.

Salaries for coaches often include pay for teaching as well. According to the *American Almanac of Jobs and Salaries 1997,* college head football coaches earn an average of $50,000. Head coaches of men's college basketball teams average $69,400 annually, while coaches of women's teams average considerably less at $42,200 a year. Many larger universities pay more. Coaches of professional teams often earn between $125,000 and $500,000. Top coaches can command million-dollar-salaries.

✦ OUTLOOK

Today's fitness boom has created many employment opportunities for people employed in sports-related occupations. Health clubs, community centers, parks and recreational facilities, and private businesses now employ sports instructors who teach everything from tennis and golf to scuba diving.

According to the US Department of Labor, this occupation will grow much faster than the average through the year 2008. Job opportunities will be greatest in urban areas. Coaching jobs at the high school and amateur level will also continue to be plentiful.

◆ TRAINING

Training and educational requirements vary, depending on the specific sport and the ability level of students being instructed. Most coaches who are associated with schools have bachelor's degrees. Many middle and high school coaches are also teachers within the school. Most instructors need to combine several years of successful experience in a particular sport with some educational background, preferably in teaching. A college degree is becoming more important as part of an instructor's background. Certification is required by many facilities.

A strong interest in sports, the ability to communicate well, and the power to motivate others are skills needed for a job in this field.

◆ EXPLORING

Try to gain as much experience as possible in any and all sports. High school and college offer great opportunities to participate in sporting events as a player, manager, or trainer. Most communities have a variety of sports programs such as Little League baseball. Get involved by volunteering as a coach, umpire, or starter. Talking with sports instructors already working in the field is another way to learn more.

◆ RESOURCES

American Alliance for Health, Physical Education, Recreation, and Dance
1900 Association Drive
Reston, VA 20191
Tel: 703-476-3400
Web: http://www.aahperd.org/

American Baseball Coaches Association
108 South University Avenue, Suite 3
Mount Pleasant, MI 48858-2327
Tel: 517-775-3300

National Association for Sport and Physical Education
1900 Association Drive
Reston, VA 20191
Tel: 800-213-7193
Web: http://www.aahperd.org/naspe/naspe-main.html

SPORTS PHYSICIANS

◆ OVERVIEW

Sports physicians treat the injuries and illnesses of athletes. They are often referred to as team physicians. Sports physicians are usually either general or orthopedic surgeons. The majority are in private practice, although those who work for professional sports teams are usually too busy for private practice.

Sports physicians evaluate athletes' fitness levels, perform physical exams, supervise conditioning and injury-prevention programs, treat injuries and perform surgery when necessary, and assist with rehabilitation after surgery.

◆ EARNINGS

The earnings of sports physicians vary widely. Sports physicians for professional individual athletes, such as figure skaters, typically earn far less than physicians for professional football or basketball teams, for example.

According to the American Medical Association, general practitioners and family practice physicians earn an annual net income of approximately $112,000, not including the fees paid to them by the athletic organizations for whom they work as team physicians. Team physicians employed full time by professional organizations can make as much as $1 million or more.

◆ OUTLOOK

In the multi-million-dollar world of professional sports, teams have a strong interest in keeping their athletes healthy. Even amateur athletes increasingly require the skills and expertise of talented sports physicians. The outlook for sports physicians remains strong: Employment in this field is expected to grow faster than the average for all occupations.

◆ TRAINING

Sports physicians must have either an MD (medical doctor) or a DO (doctor of osteopathy) degree. Each involves completing four years of college, followed by four years of medical school, study and internship at an accredited medical school, and up to six years of residency training in a medical specialty, such as surgery. Many physicians also complete a fellowship in sports medicine either during or after their residency.

To become licensed, doctors must have completed the above training in accordance with the guidelines and rules of their chosen area or specialty, which usually includes a written and oral exam.

◆ EXPLORING

High school students interested in becoming sports physicians should look into working with the physician, coach, or athletic trainer for one of their school's teams. Firsthand experience on the sidelines or in a medical office is the best way to gain insight into the role of team physicians.

◆ RESOURCES

American College of Sports Medicine
PO Box 1440
Indianapolis, IN 46206-1440
Tel: 317-637-9200
Web: http://www.a1.com/sportsmed/index.html

American Orthopaedic Society for Sports Medicine
6300 North River Road, Suite 200
Rosemont, IL 60018
Tel: 847-292-4900
Web: http://www.sportsmed.org

National Athletic Trainers Association
2952 Stemmons Freeway
Dallas, TX 75247-6196
Tel: 214-637-6282
Web: http://www.nata.org

SPORTS PSYCHOLOGISTS

OVERVIEW

Sports psychologists work with amateur and professional athletes to improve their health and athletic performance through goal setting, imagery, attentional focus strategies, and relaxation techniques.

Sports psychologists work with both individual athletes and entire teams. They concentrate on the problems an athlete is having that affect his or her performance, from a bad slump to depression to drug or substance abuse. In working with teams, they help to create a feeling of cohesion among the different personalities. Team members are also counseled when they are traded to another team or released.

Sports psychologists work in one of three categories: clinical, educational, or research.

EARNINGS

Specific salary figures for sports psychologists are not readily available, but psychologists earn between $20,000 and $200,000, depending the area of their expertise and the location and size of their practice. With a higher salary, however, comes long years of study, both to get educated and licensed and to stay abreast of current developments in the field once in practice.

◆ OUTLOOK

While employment in the field of psychology in general is likely to grow more slowly than the average for all occupations through the year 2008, it is unclear how this prognosis affects the specialty of sports psychology. Competition is tough for positions with elite athletes, but experts predict that sports psychology will continue to offer opportunities for new graduates, especially in academic settings.

◆ TRAINING

One of two doctoral degrees is generally required for employment as a psychologist: a PhD, which qualifies psychologists for a wide range of teaching, research, clinical, and counseling positions in universities, elementary and secondary schools, and private industry, or a PsyD (doctor of psychology), which qualifies psychologists mainly for clinical positions.

Individuals who have only a master's degree in psychology are allowed to administer tests as psychological assistants and, under supervision, can conduct research in laboratories, perform psychological evaluations, counsel patients, teach in high schools and two-year colleges, and work as school psychologists or counselors.

Most states require that all practitioners of psychology meet certification or licensing requirements if they are in independent practice or involved in offering patient care of any kind.

EXPLORING

You can gain experience in this field by volunteering to work for research programs at area universities or by working in the office of a psychologist. Another option is to work as an intern with the sports medicine department of a college, university, or professional athletic team. Even by participating in a sport in high school or college, you can gain valuable insight into the mental and emotional stresses and demands placed upon athletes.

RESOURCES

Association for the Advancement of Applied Sports Psychology

Department of Psychology
The University of Memphis
Memphis, TN 38152-6400
Web: http://www.aaasponline.org/

American Psychological Association

750 First Street, NE
Washington, DC 20002-4242
Tel: 202-336-5500
Web: http://www.apa.org

Division 47 Administrative Office

750 First Street, NE
Washington, DC 20002-4242
Tel: 202-336-6013
Web: http://www.psyc.unt.edu/apadiv47

SPORTS PUBLICISTS

 OVERVIEW

There are two types of *sports publicists:* those who work for professional and amateur teams and those who work for individual professional athletes. Sports team publicists handle the daily press operations for a sports organization. They handle media relations, including writing press releases and setting up news conferences and interviews with players. They also generate all of the team's publications, including programs, schedules, direct-mail pieces, and newsletters. In addition, they often oversee game management and special promotions.

Sports publicists who work for individual players try to enhance their clients' images by casting them in a positive light via newspaper, magazine, and television stories. They also work to create news events around their clients and schedule charity appearances for them.

EARNINGS

Sports publicists can earn anywhere from $28,000 to more than $100,000 per year. Publicists just starting out make less, while those with proven track records command higher salaries. Publicists who work for individual athletes can earn more money.

✦ OUTLOOK

The US Department of Labor predicts that employment of public relations specialists in general is expected to increase faster than average for all occupations through the year 2008, but the number of applicants with degrees in the communications fields—journalism, public relations, and advertising—is expected to exceed the number of job openings. The field of sports publicity is very competitive, and even though it is expanding as more teams and leagues form, it is still difficult to land a job.

✦ TRAINING

Because you will be the mouthpiece of the person or team that you represent, it is very important that you are an effective communicator. Take classes in English and journalism to hone your writing skills and speech to help you learn how to convey your thoughts to an audience.

According to the Public Relations Society of America, a college degree is essential for a job as a sports publicist. Most publicists working in the sports industry have college degrees in public relations, marketing, communications, journalism, or sports administration.

 EXPLORING

Ask your teacher or counselor to set up an informational interview with a sports publicist. Volunteer to handle various public relations-type duties for one of your high school sports teams or clubs.

 RESOURCE

Public Relations Society of America
33 Irving Place
New York, NY 10003-2376
Tel: 212-995-2230
Web: http://www.prsa.org

SPORTS SCOUTS

OVERVIEW

Sports scouts attend and observe sporting events for the purpose of recruiting players and gathering information about opponents' players and strategies. Most scouts work for professional sports teams.

A scout may see 10 or more games a week and must keep detailed notes on each one. Scouts examine baseball statistics like earned run average, football stats like yards per carry, or basketball stats like field goal percentage. They report their findings back to the coach or general manager, and it is up to that person to act on the scout's recommendations.

A relatively new concept in the industry is pool scouting, which involves a group of scouts who collect data on many players and provide that information to several teams. The scouts are not employed by any one team but by professional scouting organizations such as the Major League Scouting Bureau.

EARNINGS

Beginning sports scouts can expect a starting salary of $18,000 or more. Sports scouts are reimbursed for travel expenses and meals and get free admission to sporting events. With three to five years' experience, a successful scout can expect to make between $30,000 and $35,000 a year. A veteran scout may earn up to $100,000 a year.

✦ OUTLOOK

There will be little change in the number of sports scouts employed in the near future in North America. As professional leagues add expansion teams and the domestic talent pool diminishes, there will probably be more opportunities for sports scouts to travel and work in foreign countries. Baseball is the sport that employs the greatest number of scouts.

✦ TRAINING

There are no educational requirements for becoming a sports scout; a high school education will give you the basic skills you need. Speech and English courses will help you communicate easily with prospects as well as relay your findings, and knowledge of another language (particularly Spanish or Japanese) will help you connect with foreign players, who are increasingly sought after by major league teams. Most scouts are former players or coaches in the particular sport they scout in.

Sports scouts are detail-oriented and methodical and have a thorough understanding of the rules, regulations, fundamentals, and strategies of their sport. They are also good judges of talent and character.

 EXPLORING

Individuals interested in a career as a sports scout should participate in sporting events at the high school and college level, either as a player or as an assistant to players or coaches. Taking part in community sports programs will allow you to interact with a variety of players and observe different styles of play. Reading books on the fundamentals and strategies of the sport you are interested in will also be helpful.

 RESOURCES

American and National League of Baseball Clubs
350 Park Avenue
New York, NY 10022
Tel: 212-339-7600

National Basketball Association
645 Fifth Avenue
New York, NY 10022
Tel: 212-826-7000
Web: http://www.nba.com/

National Football League
410 Park Avenue
New York, NY 10022
Tel: 212-758-1500

SPORTS STATISTICIANS

◇ OVERVIEW

Sports statisticians compute and record the statistics for sporting events, games, or competitions or on the accomplishments of a team or single athlete during competition. They use basic math and algebraic formulas, manually or in combination with calculators and computers, to calculate the statistics related to a particular sport or athlete.

The statistician at a basketball game, for example, keeps track of the score, the number of time-outs, and specific calls made by the referees, such as team and player fouls. The statistician is also referred to as the official scorer because if any item on the scoreboard is questioned—by a referee, one of the coaches, or another game official—the individual who ultimately has the power to determine the outcome is the statistician.

Statisticians may work for a school or athletic team, a television or radio station, or a private company.

◇ EARNINGS

Salaries depend largely on the level of athletics in which the statistician is involved. For example, a statistician working freelance for a local radio station might receive $25 per game, whereas a statistician working freelance for one of the large television networks, like Fox TV, might receive between $400 and $500 per game. Many statisticians must work full-time jobs, often in totally unrelated fields, in order to support themselves.

On the other hand, statisticians who work full-time for radio and television receive salaries commensurate with jobs in other fields. An individual working with one of these companies might earn $25,000 to $35,000 after one to five years, $35,000 to $50,000 for five to 10 years, and up to $100,000 beyond that.

✦ OUTLOOK

Increased sports coverage through cable television and satellite reception, plus developing technologies and markets on the Internet, will only increase the demand for sports statistics and the individuals who record and catalogue them. But competition for full-time statistician jobs is stiff. Those who currently have full-time positions in sports statistics aren't likely to leave those jobs. Attrition rates due to retirement and advancement, combined with new jobs, should keep this field developing just slightly faster than the average.

T R A I N I N G

Technically, there are no formal educational requirements for the job of sports statistician. However, private companies that employ sports statisticians usually require candidates to have a bachelor's degree in a related field, such as marketing, accounting, communications, or sports administration. Knowing how to manually score a game or event, and knowing as much as possible about the sport or sports for which you would like to keep statistics, are the basic requirements, as well as a solid grasp of math and computers.

 E X P L O R I N G

The best way to gain experience in this field is to learn as much as possible about how a sport is played and how to score it, especially sports that you enjoy most. High school and college students can easily accomplish this by participating in sports or volunteering to act as statistician for one of the teams.

There are books available for nearly every sport that explain in detail how to correctly keep statistics. Talking to a veteran scorer at a local baseball or basketball game is another good way to learn about the process. These people are also good contacts to have when looking for a job in the field.

R E S O U R C E S

Elias Sports Bureau
500 Fifth Avenue, 21st Floor
New York, NY 10110
Tel: 212-869-1530

ESPN/Sportsticker
Harborside Financial Center
600 Plaza Two
Jersey City, NJ 07311

Stats, Inc.
8130 Lehigh Avenue
Morton Grove, IL 60053
Tel: 847-677-3322
Web: http://www.stats.com

SPORTS TRAINERS

✦ OVERVIEW

Sports trainers—also referred to as *athletic trainers, certified sports medicine trainers,* and *certified sports medicine therapists*—are concerned with preventing injuries to amateur and professional athletes through proper exercises and conditioning; providing immediate first aid for injuries as they occur during a practice, game, or competition; and leading injured athletes safely through rehabilitation programs and routines.

For the most part, athletic trainers are not medical doctors, but they regularly consult with physicians during all stages of athletic training to ensure that athletes under their care are physically capable of participating in competition. Sports trainers may specialize in health care administration, education, or counseling.

✦ EARNINGS

Earnings vary depending on the level of athletics in which the trainer is involved, the trainer's education and credentials, and the type of his or her responsibilities. In general, sports trainers who are just entering the field should expect to earn salaries in the mid-twenties. Trainers who work with college athletes may earn slightly more, and trainers with more experience and responsibility earn between $40,000 and $80,000 annually. Only in rare instances will a trainer earn more than $80,000 a year.

✦ OUTLOOK

The outlook for athletic trainers depends on the level of athletics in which the trainer is involved, but the field as a whole is expected to grow faster than the average. Competition for the more glamorous jobs is tough; positions with professional athletes and teams are extremely difficult to find and those working in them usually have years of experience. Positions at the college and university level offer the athletic trainer greater stability, since there is little turnover. Competition for these spots is also tough, however, and many schools are now requiring candidates to have a master's degree in order to be considered. More opportunities exist for the certified athletic trainer who works with high school athletes, especially if the trainer also teaches a high school subject like math, science, or physical education.

✦ TRAINING

Most sports trainers have a bachelor's degree from a college or university with an accredited athletic training program. Some also earn master's degrees in a related health field.

Athletic trainers in charge of every level of athlete should be licensed to perform specific medical functions and operate certain devices and equipment. Different membership organizations and their respective certifying bodies have different eligibility requirements.

Workers in this field also need an understanding of human anatomy and physiology and should not be panicky or squeamish when it comes to handling medical emergencies. They should be compassionate and able to communicate well in high-pressure situations.

✦ EXPLORING

High school and college students can gain valuable experience by actively participating in a sport. Such experience gives insight into the injuries typical of a given sport, as well as compassion and empathy for injured athletes who are forced to sit out a game. Most teams need help with everything from equipment to statistics, so there are plenty of opportunities to participate even if you do not compete or play yourself. You can often work with a trainer or team physician, learning beside a professional.

✦ RESOURCES

American Athletic Trainers Association & Certification Board
660 West Duarte Road, Suite 1
Arcadia, CA 91007
Tel: 818-445-1978

American Sports Medicine Association
660 West Duarte Road, Suite 1
Arcadia, CA 91007
Tel: 818-445-1978

National Athletic Trainers Association
2952 Stemmons Freeway
Dallas, TX 75247-6196
Tel: 214-637-6282
Web: http://www.nata.org

SPORTSWRITERS

◆ OVERVIEW

Sportswriters write news and feature articles on sports for newspapers and magazines. They research original ideas for features, follow up on breaking stories, or cover games or competitions, contacting coaches, athletes, team owners and managers, and others for comments and information. Sometimes a sportswriter is fortunate enough to get his or her own column, in which the sportswriter editorializes on current news or developments in sports. Most newspaper sportswriters are assigned a "beat" or specialize in one particular sport. Magazine sportswriters are more likely to cover a range of sports and athletes.

EARNINGS

According the *Occupational Outlook Handbook,* the median minimum salary for new reporters was about $448 a week in 1996, or $23,036 annually. The median minimum weekly salary for reporters after three to six years on the job was about $742 a week.

Sportswriters who cover major sporting events, who have their own column, or who write for major magazines can expect to earn much more than the salaries above.

◆ OUTLOOK

Competition for sportswriting jobs will continue to be strong into the year 2008 and beyond. The turnover rate for top sportswriters with major newspapers and magazines isn't very high, which means that job openings occur as sportswriters retire, die, are fired, or move into other markets.

TRAINING

English, journalism, and speech are the most important high school classes for an aspiring sportswriter. Participation in and exposure to sports, both in high school and college, is also highly useful. A bachelor's degree is usually the minimum level of education required of sportswriters, although many go on to study journalism at the graduate level. A journalism degree is recommended, as competition in the sportswriting field is incredibly fierce.

To be a sportswriter, you must be able to write clearly and concisely, have a solid understanding of the rules and fundamentals of many different sports, and have the ability to be assertive in pursuing information.

✦ EXPLORING

You can learn on-the-job skills by working for your high school and college newspapers. The experience can be related to sports, of course, but any journalistic experience will help you develop basic reporting skills.

You can increase your chances and success in the field by applying to colleges or universities with renowned academic programs in journalism. Most accredited programs have a required period of training as an intern with a major US newspaper; student interns are responsible for covering a beat.

✦ RESOURCE

Newspaper Association of America
1921 Gallows Road, Suite 600
Vienna, VA 22182
Tel: 703-902-1600
Web: http://www.naa.org/

UMPIRES AND REFEREES

◆ OVERVIEW

Umpires and *referees* ensure that competitors in athletic events follow the rules and guidelines of their sport. They observe players while the ball or other apparatus is in play and penalize those who break the rules. Umpires and referees are the decision makers and the arbiters of disputes between the competing teams.

When an infraction of the rules is spotted by an official, the official blows a whistle to stop play. The penalty is communicated to the official scorer, the penalty is assessed, and play continues.

Officiating jobs are available in many different sports, but some of the more common jobs are baseball umpires, basketball referees, and football referees.

The duties of an official vary greatly from sport to sport because each has its own set of rules and regulations. Even the same game played on different levels may have its own distinct rules. For example, in professional basketball, the team in possession of the ball has 24 seconds to take a shot on goal. On the college level, the shot clock is set at 45 seconds, and for most high school teams, there is no shot clock at all.

◆ EARNINGS

Umpire and referee salaries vary greatly, depending upon the sport and the level at which it is played.

According to the Major League Baseball's Umpire Development Program, 1997 umpire salaries ranged from $2,000 per month in the Rookie League to $3,400 per month in the Triple-A League to a starting annual salary of about $70,000 for a Major League umpire. Major League umpires with considerable experience can earn as much as $181,000 a year. Professional basketball officials' salaries started at about $77,000 a year in 1997, according to an NBA spokesman, and rose significantly with experience. The National Football League cited 1997 salaries from $2,100 to $4,000 per game, depending on experience.

Umpires and referees at the college, amateur, and youth levels are paid by the game. College officials earn between $200 and $800 per game, and high school and middle school officials earn considerably less.

✦ OUTLOOK

The outlook for the field of sports officiating depends upon the sport and the league worked. Umpires and referees are almost always needed at the youth, high school, and amateur levels, and people who are interested in supplementing their incomes this way or simply learning about the field of officiating should find plenty of opportunities.

In professional sports the market is much tighter. Umpires in Major League Baseball rarely leave the job except to retire. When an opening does occur, an umpire moves up from Triple-A, creating an opening for an umpire from Double-A, and so on. Professional sports without minor leagues offer even fewer employment opportunities for officials at the professional level, but the creation of new leagues and expansion teams does offer additional job opportunities for professional sports officials.

The outlook for women sports officials has improved in recent years with the addition of women officials in the National Basketball Association, as well as the creation of the Women's National Basketball Association and other women's professional sports organizations.

✦ TRAINING

While umpires and referees are not required to attend four-year colleges or universities, many do have college degrees. Attending college and participating in college athletics is an excellent way to reinforce your knowledge of a sport and its rules, while at the same time receiving a solid education.

In almost all cases, officials must attend special training schools or courses. These can range from schools endorsed by the Major League's Umpire Development Program to training courses for amateur softball officials. These schools and training courses can be contacted through professional and amateur leagues, college athletic conferences, and state interscholastic commissions.

Strong communication skills, the ability to be diplomatic with people of varying backgrounds, good physical health and stamina, and the ability to remain calm under pressure are basic requirements for the job.

✦ EXPLORING

A great way to find out if you enjoy being an umpire or referee is to officiate for a Little League team, summer camp, or amateur league. Try to locate a sports official in your area and set up an informational interview. Watch and participate in athletic activities as often as you can to learn more about the fundamentals of various sports.

◆ **RESOURCES**

International Association of Approved Basketball Officials
12321 Middlebrook Road
Germantown, MD 20875
Web: http://www.iaabo.org/

Jim Evans Academy of Professional Umpiring
12741 Research Boulevard, Suite 401
Austin, TX 78759
Tel: 512-335-5959
Web: http://www.umpireacademy.com

Major League Umpires Association
Mellon Bank Center
1735 Market Street, Suite 3420
Philadelphia, PA 19103
Web: http://www.majorleagueumps.com/

National Association of Sports Officials
2017 Lathrop Avenue
Racine, WI 53405
Tel: 414-632-5448
Web: http://www.naso.org/

CHAPTER 2

Community Service

> *We like to see well-rounded, self-directed students who care enough to be involved in their schools and communities.*
>
> – Lisa Mauldin, Senior Admissions Counselor,
> Prescott College, Prescott, Arizona

✦ INTRODUCTION

Do you like to work with other people and make a difference in their lives? This chapter will show you some of the opportunities you have, through your career, to help people who are disadvantaged or struggling in some way.

As you read through these articles, consider how you might fit into one of the roles described. Perhaps you are a good listener for friends who are having problems and feel social work is something you'd like to explore. If you feel comfortable in the company of your grandparents or older neighbors, a career as an adult day care coordinator might sound interesting.

Whether it's teaching people new skills, helping them to cope with an addiction, or caring for the sick, community service work is critically needed in our society today. And careers in community service can be deeply rewarding.

Helping others to help themselves could be your calling.

ADULT DAY CARE COORDINATORS

◆ OVERVIEW

Adult day care coordinators direct day care programs for adults—usually elderly or disabled—who cannot be left alone during the day. They oversee staff members who provide medical and physical care, meals, and social activities for clients. A typical staff might include a nurse, a physical therapist, a social worker, a cook, and several aides. Coordinators are responsible for staff hiring, training, and scheduling, as well as planning, scheduling, and budgeting for daily and weekly activities. They also serve as liaison between the day care center and its clients' families. Coordinators at small facilities sometimes work directly with the clients. They also have a wider range of responsibilities, including such tasks as purchasing and inventory.

◆ EARNINGS

Starting salaries for this position depend on the experience and education of the coordinator and the size and location of the day care center. Larger centers located in metropolitan areas tend to offer the highest wages.

According to the Association for Gerontology in Higher Education, beginning annual salaries range from $18,000 to $31,000 for persons with a bachelor's degree and little experience. Experienced coordinators with a bachelor's degree employed in large, well-funded centers may earn from $20,000 to $45,000 annually.

◆ OUTLOOK

The career outlook for adult day care coordinators, as for all human services workers, is expected to be excellent through the year 2008. According to the US Department of Labor, the number of human services workers is projected to grow by 53 percent between the years 1998 and 2008, with adult day care being one of the fastest-growing subfields.

The main reason for this is that the senior citizen population is growing rapidly. Currently, there are 34 million Americans over the age of 65; by 2030, there will be more than 69 million. According to the National Adult Day Services Association, there were as few as 15 adult day care centers in existence in the 1970s; today there are more than 4,000. This growth should continue as Americans become increasingly aware of the diverse needs of the elderly. Adult day care is expected to be used more frequently as a cost-efficient and preferable alternative to nursing homes.

TRAINING

Although most employers require at least a high school diploma, there are no definite educational requirements for becoming an adult day care coordinator. Some people learn their skills on the job; others have taken courses in home nursing or health care.

Many employers prefer to hire candidates who meet the standards set by the National Adult Day Services Association. In order to meet these standards, a coordinator must have a bachelor's degree in health or social services or a related field, with one year of supervisory experience in a social or health services setting. In preparation for such a career, a college student might choose occupational, recreational, or rehabilitation therapy or social work. An increasingly popular major for potential adult day care coordinators is gerontology, or geriatrics.

Personal characteristics necessary for success in this field include compassion and the desire to help others as well as an affinity for the elderly and disabled.

 # EXPLORING

There are several ways for high school students to learn more about the career of adult day care coordinator. The easiest way is to visit a nursing home or adult day care center in order to experience firsthand what the environment is like. A volunteer or part-time position in such a facility would allow you to gauge your aptitude for working with the elderly. You might also check your local library for books or articles on aging.

RESOURCES

American Association of Homes and Services for the Aging
901 E Street, NW, Suite 500
Washington, DC 20004-2011
Tel: 202-783-2242
Web: http://www.aahsa.org

American Geriatrics Society
770 Lexington Avenue, Suite 300
New York, NY 10021
Tel: 212-308-1414
Web: http://www.americangeriatrics.org

Gerontological Society of America
1030 15th Street, NW, Suite 250
Washington, DC 20005-1503
Tel: 202-842-1275
Web: http://www.geron.org

National Adult Day Services Association
National Council on Aging
409 Third Street, SW, Suite 200
Washington, DC 20024
Tel: 202-479-6682
Web: http://www.ncoa.org/nadsa

HOME HEALTH CARE AIDES

◆ OVERVIEW

Home health care aides, also known as *homemaker-home health aides* or *home attendants,* serve elderly and infirm persons by visiting them in their homes and caring for them. Working under the supervision of nurses and/or social workers, they perform various household chores and errands that clients are unable to perform for themselves and attend to their personal and health needs. These include giving medications and dietary supplements, monitoring temperatures and pulse rates, changing dressings, operating special equipment such as hydraulic lifts, assisting with braces or artificial limbs, and helping with exercises and other therapies such as massages and whirlpool baths. Although they work primarily with the elderly, home health care aides also attend to clients with disabilities, parents needing help with small children, and people who are recovering at home following hospitalization.

◆ EARNINGS

Earnings for home health care aides are commensurate with salaries in related health care positions. For many aides who begin as part-time employees, the starting salary is usually the minimum hourly wage. For full-time aides with significant training or experience, earnings may be around $6 to $8 per hour. According to the US Department of Labor, Medicare-certified aides earned an hourly average of $7.58 in 1998. Aides are usually paid only for the time worked in the home; they normally are not paid for travel time between jobs.

◆ OUTLOOK

As government and private agencies develop more programs to assist the dependent, the need for home health care aides will continue to grow much faster than the average. Because of the physical and emotional demands of the job, there is high turnover and, therefore, frequent job openings for home health care aides.

Also, the number of people 70 years of age and older is expected to increase substantially, and many of them will require at least some home care. Rising health care costs are causing many insurance companies to consider alternatives to hospital treatment, so many insurance providers now cover home care services. In addition, hospitals and nursing homes are trying to balance the demand for their services and their limitations in staff and physical facilities. The availability of home health care aides can allow such institutions to offer quality care to more people.

✦ TRAINING

Many programs require only a high school diploma for entry-level positions. Most agencies will offer free training to prospective employees. Training is usually focused on first aid, hygiene, and the principles of health care. Cooking and nutrition, including meal preparation for patients with specific dietary needs, are often included in the program. Also included are sessions on how to bathe, dress, and feed patients as well as how to help them climb stairs and get out of bed. Home health care aides may take courses in psychology and child development as well as family living.

The federal government has enacted guidelines for home health aides whose employers receive reimbursement from Medicare. Under these guidelines, all aides must pass a competency test.

Home health care aides perform physically demanding work; lifting clients, doing housework, and assisting with physical therapy all require that an aide be in good physical condition. An even temperament, a willingness to serve others, and a high level of respect, sensitivity, and patience are important characteristics for home health care aides. Cheerfulness and a sense of humor can also go a long way in establishing a good relationship with a client.

✦ EXPLORING

Home health care aides are employed in many different areas. Interested students can learn more about the work by contacting local agencies and programs that provide home care services and requesting information on the organization's employment guidelines and training programs. Visiting the county or city health department and contacting the personnel director may be helpful as well. Local organizations often sponsor open houses to educate the community about the services they provide. This could be an excellent opportunity to meet the staff involved and learn about job opportunities. You might even be able to accompany a home health care aide on a home visit.

✦ RESOURCES

National Association of Health Career Schools
750 First Street, NE, Suite 940
Washington, DC 20002
Web: http://www.nahcs.org

National HomeCaring Council
Tel: 202-547-6586

HUMAN SERVICES WORKERS

◆ OVERVIEW

Under the direction of *social workers, psychologists, sociologists,* and other professionals, *human services workers* offer support to families, the elderly, the poor, and others in need. They are employed by government agencies, shelters, halfway houses, schools, community centers, and hospitals. They may work as aides, assistants, technicians, or counselors, working individually with clients or in group counseling. For example, a human services worker might teach life and communication skills to people in mental health facilities or offer encouragement and support to people in substance abuse programs. They also direct clients to social services and benefits and serve as advocates for them.

◆ EARNINGS

Salaries of human services workers depend in part on their employer and amount of experience. According to the *Occupational Outlook Handbook,* starting salaries for human services workers averaged about $21,360 a year. Experienced workers can earn more than $33,840 annually.

◆ OUTLOOK

Employment for human services workers will grow much faster than the average through 2008. Much of this growth is expected to occur in homes for the mentally impaired and developmentally disabled. Also, the life expectancy for people in the United States continues to rise, which will require more assistance for the elderly, such as adult day care and meal delivery. Correctional facilities are also expected to employ many more human services workers. Because counseling inmates and offenders can be somewhat undesirable work, there are a number of high-paying jobs available in that area.

Job prospects in public agencies are not as bright as they once were because of fiscal policies that tighten eligibility requirements for federal welfare and other payments. State and local governments are expected to remain major employers, however, as the burden of providing social services is shifted from the federal government to the state and local level.

◆ TRAINING

Some employers will hire people with only a high school education, but these employees might find it hard to move beyond clerical positions. Certificate and associate degree programs in human services or mental health are offered at community and junior colleges, vocational-technical institutes, and other postsecondary institutions. It is also possible to pursue a bachelor's degree in human services. Undergraduate and graduate programs typically include courses in psychology, sociology, crisis intervention, family dynamics, therapeutic interviewing, rehabilitation, and gerontology.

A genuine interest in the well-being of others and a sensitivity to their situations is important to a human services worker. In addition to the rewarding aspects of the job, a human services worker must be prepared to take on difficult responsibilities. Because the work can be stressful, patience and an even temperament are very important.

◆ EXPLORING

To get an idea of the requirements of human service, try volunteering at a local service agency or institution. Churches and other religious centers also involve young people in volunteer work, as do the Red Cross, the Boy Scouts, and the Girl Scouts. Opportunities might include reading to the blind, visiting with residents of a nursing home, or helping out at a homeless shelter.

Some members of high school organizations also perform social services within their own schools, educating classmates on the dangers of gangs, unsafe sex, and substance abuse. By contributing to your community, you can gain experience in the field as well as build up a history of volunteer service that will impress future employers.

◆ RESOURCES

American Association for Counseling and Development
5999 Stevenson Avenue
Alexandria, VA 22304
Tel: 800-545-2223

Council for Standards in Human Service Education
Northern Essex Community College
Haverhill, MA 01830

National Organization for Human Service Education
5326 Avery Road
New Port Richey, FL 34652
Tel: 727-847-7533
Web: http://www.nohse.com/

REHABILITATION COUNSELORS

✦ OVERVIEW

Rehabilitation counselors work with people with disabilities to identify barriers to medical, psychological, personal, social, and vocational adjustment and develop a plan of action to remove or reduce those barriers. They provide counseling and guidance services to help their clients resolve life problems; live independently; and train for and find work that is suitable to their physical and mental abilities, interests, and aptitudes.

✦ EARNINGS

Information about salaries for rehabilitation counselors is limited. Salaries vary widely according to each state and community, averaging around $20,000 per year. Rehabilitation counselors with many years of experience can earn up to $50,000 per year. Those in supervisory and administrative positions can earn up to $65,000 per year. Self-employed counselors with established practices generally earn the highest salaries.

Rehabilitation counselors employed by the federal government generally start at the GS-9 or GS-11 level. In 2000, the GS-9 level salary was between $32,380 and $42,091. Those with master's degrees generally began at the GS-11 level, with a starting salary of $39,178.

✦ OUTLOOK

This field is expected to grow faster than the average in the near future. The passage of the Americans with Disabilities Act of 1990 has increased the demand for rehabilitation counselors through the year 2008, as more local, state, and federal programs are initiated that are designed to assist people with disabilities, and as private institutions and companies seek to comply with this new legislation. Budget pressures may serve to limit the numbers of new rehabilitation counselors hired by government agencies; however, the overall outlook remains excellent.

✦ TRAINING

Although there are some positions available for people with a bachelor's degree in rehabilitation counseling, a master's degree in rehabilitation counseling, counseling and guidance, or counseling psychology is preferred for those entering the field. Preparation for a master's degree program requires an undergraduate major in behavioral sciences, social sciences, or a related field or the completion of an undergraduate degree program in rehabilitation counseling. Many large universities also have graduate programs in rehabilitation counseling.

Most state government rehabilitation agencies, which employ about 40 percent of all rehabilitation counselors, require future counselors to meet state civil service and merit system rules. Many employers now require their rehabilitation counselors to be certified by the Commission on Rehabilitation Counselor Certification. In about 45 states, counselors in private practice must be licensed by the state.

The most important personal attribute required for rehabilitation counseling is the ability to get along well with other people. Work in this field also requires patience, persistence, and a positive attitude.

◆ EXPLORING

Students considering a career working with people with disabilities should seek opportunities to work in this field. You might volunteer to work as a counselor at a camp for disabled children or with a local vocational rehabilitation agency or group like the Easter Seal Society. You could also pursue reading to the blind or teaching a hobby to someone who has been disabled by an accident or illness.

◆ RESOURCES

American Rehabilitation Counseling Association
c/o American Counseling Association
5999 Stevenson Avenue
Alexandria, VA 22304
Tel: 703-823-9800
Web: http://www.counseling.org

Commission on Rehabilitation Counselor Certification
1835 Rohlwing Road, Suite E
Rolling Meadows, IL 60008
Tel: 847-394-2104

National Rehabilitation Counseling Association
8807 Sudley Road, Suite 102
Manassas, VA 22110-4719
Tel: 703-361-2077
Web: http://www.nchrtm.okstate.edu/ARCA/

SOCIAL WORKERS

✦ OVERVIEW

Social workers help people and communities overcome the challenges of poverty, discrimination, physical and mental illness, addiction, and abuse. They are dedicated to empowering people and helping them to preserve their dignity and worth. Those in direct social work (about three-quarters of all social workers) offer counseling—both for groups and individuals—as well as advocacy, information and referral, and education. Those in indirect practice—typically social workers who hold PhDs—are involved in program development and evaluation, administration, research, and policy analysis. Common areas of specialty include health care/mental health, child care/family services, gerontology, and school social work.

✦ EARNINGS

The higher your degree, the more money you can make in the social work profession. Your area of practice also determines earnings. The areas of mental health, group services, and community organization and planning offer higher salaries, while elderly and disabled care generally offer lower pay.

The median salary range for social workers in the United States is approximately $35,000 for those with a MSW. Those who hold a bachelor's degree earn about $25,000 a year. Social workers employed by the US government earn an average annual salary of about $46,900.

Although women make up a large percentage of the profession, only 2.2 percent of female social workers in the United States receive more than $60,000, as opposed to 6.3 percent of male social workers in that category.

✦ OUTLOOK

The field of social work is expected to grow much faster than the average for all occupations through 2008. The greatest factor for this growth is the increased number of older people who are in need of social services. Social workers that specialize in gerontology will find many job opportunities in nursing homes, hospitals, and home health care agencies.

Schools will also need more social workers; however, job availability in schools will depend on funding provided by state and local sources.

To help control costs, hospitals are encouraging early discharge for some of their patients. Social workers will be needed to help secure health services for these patients in their homes.

Competition for jobs in urban areas will remain strong. However, there is still a shortage of social workers in rural areas; these areas usually cannot offer the high salaries or modern facilities that attract large numbers of applicants.

◆ TRAINING

Although some work is available in this field for those with only a high school diploma or associate degree, the most opportunities exist for people with degrees in social work. Most bachelor's degree programs require two years of liberal arts study followed by two years of study in the social work major and a field practicum. Most supervisory and administrative positions require at least an MSW. Doctoral degrees prepare students for research and teaching. Many social workers with doctorates go to work in community organizations.

Licensing, certification, or registration of social workers is required by all states. To receive the necessary licensing, a social worker typically has to gain a certain amount of experience and also pass an exam.

Social work requires great dedication. You must remain sensitive to the problems of your clients, offering support and not moral judgment or personal bias. An open mind, a clarity of vision, and a genuine concern for the well-being of others are all needed to be successful in this field. Along with the rewards that can come from this position, the work can be stressful and at times discouraging, so social workers also must be patient, persistent, and optimistic.

◆ EXPLORING

As a high school student, you might seek openings for summer, part-time, or volunteer work as a receptionist or file clerk with a local social service agency. Work as a counselor in a camp for children with physical, mental, or developmental disabilities also will offer good experience. Your local YMCA, park district, or other recreational facility may need volunteers for group recreation programs, including programs designed for the prevention of delinquency. You could also volunteer a few afternoons a week to read to people in retirement homes or to the blind. And work as a tutor in special education programs is sometimes available to high school students.

By reporting for your high school newspaper, you'll have the opportunity to interview people, conduct surveys, and do research, all of which can provide good experience for prospective social workers who are considering indirect practice.

◆ RESOURCES

Canadian Association of Schools of Social Work

383 Parkdale Avenue, Suite 206
Ottawa, ON K1Y 4R4, Canada
Tel: 613-729-1953
Web: http://www.cassw-acess.ca/

Council on Social Work Education

1600 Duke Street, Suite 300
Alexandria, VA 22314
Tel: 703-683-8080
Web: http://www.cswe.org

National Association of Social Workers

Career Information
750 First Street, NE, Suite 700
Washington DC 20002-4241
Tel: 202-408-8600
Web: http://www.naswdc.org

"*I would encourage students to find one to two activities that they can maintain a commitment to through their high school career. This stick-to-itiveness tells us a great deal about their ability to commit to a goal or an objective.* **"**

— Dan Meyer, Dean of Admission,
St. Norbert College, DePere, Wisconsin

"*Extracurricular activities and accomplishments play an especially important role in the selection of students at highly competitive, residential liberal arts colleges. Our aim as an admissions committee is to build a campus community that is highly involved, highly interactive, diverse, and accomplished. The best way to predict an applicant's potential for contribution outside of class in college is to assess that candidate's engagement in activities outside of class in high school.* **"**

— Parker Beverage, Dean of Admissions and Financial Aid,
Colby College, Waterville, Maine

CHAPTER 3

Computer Clubs

> *"Extracurricular activities are important.*
> *They help us to understand the fabric of the applicant.* "*
>
> – *Michael Steidel, Director of Admission,*
> *Carnegie Mellon, Pittsburgh, Pennsylvania*

✦ INTRODUCTION

Computer was the name once given to people who performed computations. Today's computers are machines that are omnipresent in our lives. From the mirochip in your alarm clock to the scanner at the supermarket checkout, almost everything we do is controlled or influenced by a computer.

The electronic revolution of the last several years has made computer-related jobs some of the fastest-growing careers around. Any job involving computers—repair, support, sales, programming, manufacturing, or research—holds great promise for the future. With technology changing so quickly, many jobs, such as those related to the Internet, are still in their infancy and are promising for the future.

If you are technically savvy and want a profession that's on the cutting edge, consider connecting to one of the careers described in this chapter.

COMPUTER PROGRAMMERS

✦ OVERVIEW

Computer programmers write, test, and maintain instructions in a computer language, or code, that tell a computer how to perform its functions. Broadly speaking, there are two types of computer programmers: *systems programmers* and *applications programmers*. Systems programmers maintain the programs and software that control an entire computer system, including the central processing unit and the equipment with which it communicates, such as terminals, printers, and disk drives. Applications programmers write the software to handle specific jobs and may specialize as engineering and scientific programmers or as business programmers.

✦ EARNINGS

According to the *Occupational Outlook Handbook,* the median annual earnings for computer programmers were $47,550 in 1998. The middle 50 percent earned between $36,020 and $70,610 a year. The lowest 10 percent earned less than $27,670; the highest 10 percent earned more than $88,730. The *Handbook* also reported that according to Robert Half International, average annual starting salaries in 1999 ranged from $38,000 to $50,500 for applications development programmers and from $49,000 to $63,000 for systems programmers.

✦ OUTLOOK

Employment opportunities for computer programmers should increase faster than the average through 2008, according to the US Department of Labor. Employment growth will be strong because businesses, scientific organizations, government agencies, and schools continue to look for new applications for computers and to make improvements in software already in use. Also, there is a need to develop complex operating programs that can use higher-level computer languages and can network with other computer equipment and systems.

Job applicants with the best chances of employment will be college graduates with a knowledge of several programming languages, especially newer ones used for computer networking and database management. Competition for jobs will be heavier among graduates of two-year data processing programs and people with equivalent experience or training.

✦ TRAINING

As the market becomes saturated with individuals wishing to break into this field, a college degree is becoming increasingly important. Many junior and community colleges offer two-year associate degree programs in data processing, computer programming, and other computer-related technologies. Most four-year colleges and universities have computer science departments with a variety of computer-related majors, any of which could prepare a student for a career in programming.

Some employers whose work is highly technical require that programmers be qualified in the area in which the firm or agency operates. Engineering firms, for example, prefer young people with an engineering background and are willing to train them in some programming techniques.

Since this field is constantly changing, programmers must stay abreast of the latest technology to remain competitive.

Personal qualifications important for a career in this field are a high degree of reasoning ability, patience, and persistence, as well as an aptitude for mathematics.

EXPLORING

It is a good idea to start early and get hands-on experience operating and programming a computer. Resources for teaching yourself are highly accessible and available for all levels of competency. Joining a computer club, reading professional magazines, and researching on the Internet are other ways to learn more.

Business computer centers and some large companies hire high school and college students for part-time work. Another way to explore this field is to visit a large bank or insurance company and make an appointment to talk with a programmer on the staff. You may be able to visit the data processing center and see the machines in operation. You could also try contacting a sales representative from a large manufacturer of data processing equipment and request any literature the company publishes.

RESOURCES

Association for Computing Machinery
One Astor Plaza
1515 Broadway
New York, NY 10036
Tel: 212-869-7440
Web: http://www.acm.org

Association of Information Technology Professionals
315 South Northwest Highway, Suite 200
Park Ridge, IL 60068-4278
Tel: 800-224-9371
Web: http://www.aitp.org

Institute for Certification of Computing Professionals
2200 East Devon Avenue, Suite 247
Des Plaines, IL 60018
Tel: 800-843-8227
Web: http://www.iccp.org

COMPUTER SYSTEMS/PROGRAMMER ANALYSTS

 OVERVIEW

Computer systems analysts plan and develop new computer systems or upgrade existing systems to meet changing business needs. Their job involves meeting with management and users to discuss their needs; using tools like structural analysis, data modeling, mathematics, and cost accounting to determine what equipment will be needed to meet the goals of a project; preparing and presenting reports to management; and, once a project is approved, purchasing, installing, programming or reprogramming, and testing the computer system. They also maintain the systems and solve problems that arise.

The position can be split between two people—the *systems analyst* and the *systems programmer*—but is frequently held by just one person who oversees the work from beginning to end.

EARNINGS

According to the *Occupational Outlook Handbook,* median annual earnings of computer systems analysts were $52,180 in 1998. The middle 50 percent earned between $40,570 and $74,180 a year. The lowest 10 percent earned less than $32,470 and the highest 10 percent earned more than $87,810. The *Handbook* listed 1997 median annual earnings for the industries employing the largest numbers of computer systems analysts as follows: telephone communications, $63,300; federal government, $56,900; computer and data processing services, $51,000; state government (except education and hospitals), $43,500; and colleges and universities, $38,400.

OUTLOOK

The US Department of Labor predicts that the occupation of computer systems/programmer analyst will be one of the three fastest-growing careers through 2008. Businesses will increasingly rely on systems/programmer analysts to make the right purchasing decisions and to keep systems running smoothly.

Many computer manufacturers are beginning to expand the range of services they offer to business clients. In the years to come, they may hire many systems/programmer analysts to work as consultants on a per-project basis with clients. And more and more independent consulting firms are hiring systems/programmer analysts to perform the same tasks.

Programmer analysts with advanced degrees in computer science, management information systems, or computer engineering will be in great demand. MBAs with emphasis in information systems will also be highly desirable.

◆ TRAINING

A bachelor's degree in computer science is a minimum requirement for systems/programmer analysts. Course work in preparation for this field includes math, computer programming, science, and logic. Several years of related work experience, including knowledge of programming languages, are often necessary as well. For some very high-level positions, an advanced degree in a specific computer subfield may be required. Also, depending on the employer, proficiency in business, science, or engineering may be necessary.

Successful systems/programmer analysts demonstrate strong analytic skills and enjoy the challenges of problem solving. They can visualize complicated and abstract relationships between computer hardware and software and are good at matching needs to equipment. Programmer analysts have to be flexible as well; they routinely deal with many different kinds of people, from management to data entry clerks.

As is true for all computer professionals, systems/programmer analysts must be able to learn about new technologies quickly.

EXPLORING

To learn more about the job of computer systems analyst, consider spending a day with someone working in the field. Career days of this type can usually be arranged through school guidance counselors or public relations managers at local corporations.

Strategy games, including chess, are a good way to exercise your analytic thinking skills while having fun.

Lastly, you should become a computer hobbyist and learn everything you can about computers. Surfing the Internet regularly and reading trade magazines will be helpful. You might also want to try hooking up a mini system at home or school, configuring terminals, printers, modems, and other peripherals into a coherent system.

RESOURCES

Association of Information Technology Professionals
315 South Northwest Highway, Suite 200
Park Ridge, IL 60068-4278

Tel: 800-224-9371

Web: http://www.aitp.org

Association for Systems Management

1433 West Bagley Road

PO Box 38370

Cleveland, OH 44138

Tel: 216-234-2930

Institute for Certification of Computing Professionals

2200 East Devon Avenue, Suite 247

Des Plaines, IL 60018

Tel: 800-843-8227

Web: http://www.iccp.org

INTERNET DEVELOPERS

✦ OVERVIEW

A *Internet developer,* also called a *Web developer* or *Web designer,* is responsible for the creation of an Internet site. Most of the time, this is a public Web site, but it can also be a private network using Internet technology. Web developers are employed by a wide range of employers from small businesses and large corporations to Internet consulting firms.

Internet content developers work with marketing, sales, advertising, and other departments to determine the overall goals and look of a Web site. Using Internet programming languages, Web design software, and other Web production tools, the developer then designs the site and writes the code necessary to run and navigate it.

✦ EARNINGS

An entry-level position in Internet development at a small company pays around $30,000. As you gain experience or move to a larger company, you might make $50,000. The top of the pay scale hits around $74,000.

Jobs in the Northeast tend to pay more than positions in the Midwest or South, and men are typically paid more than women, although this may change as the number of women moving into the field gains ground on the number of men employed in these jobs.

✦ OUTLOOK

This field, like the Internet itself, is growing much faster than the average, and the outlook is promising. As more and more companies look to bring their products, services, and corporate images to the Internet, they need employees who have the ability and expertise to develop Web sites. In addition, companies are increasingly expanding internationally, creating an even greater need to be on the Web. Web developers can expect Internet technology to continue to evolve and change at a rapid pace.

✦ TRAINING

Internet developers typically hold bachelor's degrees in computer science or computer programming—although some have degrees in noncomputer areas, such as marketing, graphic design, or information systems. Regardless of educational background, you need to have an understanding of computers and computer networks and a knowledge of Internet programming languages. Formal college training in these languages may be hard to come by because of the rapid evolution of the Internet—what's hot today might be obsolete tomorrow. Because of this volatility, most postsecondary training comes from hands-on experience. This is best achieved through internships or entry-level positions.

A good Internet developer balances the technological know-how with creativity. You must be able to make a site stand out from the sea of other sites on the Web. In this job, you also must be able to adapt quickly to change. It is not uncommon to learn a new programming language, get comfortable using it, and then have to learn another new language. If you're a quick study, you should do well in this field.

◆ EXPLORING

There are many ways to learn more about the career of Internet developer. You can read trade magazines or surf the Web for information about Internet careers. You can also visit a variety of Web sites to study what makes them appealing or not so appealing. Does your high school have a Web site? If so, get involved in the planning and creation of new content for it. If not, talk to your computer teachers about creating one. You can also create your own site at home.

◆ RESOURCES

Association of Internet Professionals
9200 Sunset Boulevard, Suite 710
Los Angeles, CA 90069
Tel: 800-JOIN-AIP
Web: http://www.association.org/index.html

IEEE Computer Society
1730 Massachusetts Avenue, NW
Washington, DC 20036-1992
Tel: 202-371-0101
Web: http://www.computer.org

SOFTWARE ENGINEERS

OVERVIEW

Software engineers define and analyze specific problems in business and industry and develop and customize computer software systems and applications that effectively solve them. For example, they may be involved in the design and development of software systems for control and automation of manufacturing, business, and management processes. Software engineers spend most of their time researching, analyzing, and solving programming problems and are less concerned with writing code for programs.

Software engineers are often responsible for a significant amount of technical writing, including project proposals, progress reports, and user manuals. They are required to meet regularly with clients in order to keep projects on track. They also may install programs, train users on them, and make arrangements for ongoing technical support.

EARNINGS

According to the *Occupational Outlook Handbook,* the median annual earnings of computer engineers—including software engineers and hardware engineers—were $61,910 in 1998. The middle 50 percent earned between $46,240 and $80,500. The lowest 10 percent earned less than $37,150 and the highest 10 percent earned more than $92,850.

Computer engineers earned the following median annual salaries in 1997 by industry: computer and office equipment, $63,700; measuring and controlling devices, $62,000; management and public relations, $59,000; computer and data processing services, $56,700; and guided missiles, space vehicles, and parts, $49,500.

◆ OUTLOOK

The field of software engineering is expected to be one of the fastest-growing occupations through the year 2008, according to the US Department of Labor. Demands made on computers increase every day and from all industries. The development of one kind of software sparks ideas for many others. In addition, the demand is growing for software programs that are user-friendly.

While the need for software engineers will remain high, computer languages are likely to change every few years and software engineers will need to attend seminars and workshops to learn new computer languages and software design.

◆ TRAINING

A high school diploma is the minimum requirement for software engineering technicians, although an associate degree is also recommended. While it is possible to advance to the position of software engineer without further education, a bachelor's or advanced degree in computer science or engineering is required for most software engineers today. Software engineers planning to work in a specific technical field, such as medicine, law, or business, should receive some formal training in that particular discipline.

Another option for individuals interested in software engineering is to pursue commercial certification. These programs are usually run by computer companies that wish to train professionals in working with their products. Classes are challenging and examinations can be rigorous. New programs are introduced every year.

Software engineers need strong communication skills in order to be able to make formal business presentations and interact with people having different levels of computer expertise. They must also be patient and highly detail oriented and work well under pressure.

◆ EXPLORING

Interested high school students should consider spending a day with a working software engineer or technician to experience the work firsthand. Your school guidance counselor can help you arrange such a visit. You also might talk to your high school computer teacher for more information.

In general, you should be intent on learning as much as possible about computers and computer software. You should learn about new developments by reading trade magazines and talking to other computer users. You also can join a computer club and surf the Web for information about working in this field.

◆ RESOURCES

Association for Computing Machinery

1515 Broadway
New York, NY 10036
Tel: 212-869-7440
Web: http://www.acm.org

IEEE Computer Society

1730 Massachusetts Avenue, NW
Washington, DC 20036-1992
Tel: 202-371-0101
Web: http://www.computer.org

Institute for Certification of Computing Professionals
2200 East Devon Avenue, Suite 247
Des Plaines, IL 60018
Tel: 800-843-8227
Web: http://www.iccp.org

Software & Information Industry Association
1730 M Street, NW, Suite 700
Washington, DC 20036-4510
Tel: 202-452-1600
Web: http://www.siia.net

TECHNICAL SUPPORT SPECIALISTS

✦ OVERVIEW

Technical support specialists investigate and work to resolve problems in the functioning of computers. They listen to customer problems, walk them through possible solutions, and write reports on the results. Technical support specialists have different duties depending on whom they assist and what they fix. The three major areas in this field are user support, technical support, and microcomputer support. Most technical support specialists perform some combination of all three.

Record keeping is crucial because designers, programmers, and engineers use technical support reports to upgrade current products and improve future ones. Some support specialists help write training manuals.

✦ EARNINGS

Median annual earnings for computer support specialists—including technical support specialists, help-desk technicians, and customer service representatives—were $37,120 in 1998, according to the US Department of Labor. The middle 50 percent earned between $28,880 and $48,810. The highest 10 percent earned more than $73,790, while the lowest 10 percent earned less than $22,930.

Computer support specialists earned the following median annual salaries in 1997 by industry: management and public relations, $37,900; computer and office equipment, $36,300; computer and data processing services, $36,300; professional and commercial equipment, $35,700; and personnel supply services, $35,200.

✦ OUTLOOK

The US Department of Labor predicts that technical support specialists will be one of the fastest-growing occupations through the year 2008. The Department forecasts huge growth—about 100 percent—of additional support jobs through the year 2008. Every time a new computer product is released on the market or another system is installed, there will inevitably be problems, which means there will be a need for technical support specialists.

But while more technical support specialists will be needed in the future, The industry can be a volatile one. Start-ups and young companies dedicated to the development of one product are most vulnerable. If you are interested in working for a computer company, you should therefore consider living in an area in which many such companies are clustered. In this way, it will be easier to find another job if necessary.

TRAINING

A high school diploma is a minimum requirement for technical support specialists, and an associate degree in a computer-related technology is recommended. There are many computer technology programs that lead to an associate degree. A specialization in PC support and administration is certainly applicable to technical support. Most computer professionals eventually need to go back to school to earn a bachelor's degree in order to keep themselves competitive in the job market and prepare themselves for promotion to other computer fields.

Technical support specialists should be patient, enjoy the challenge of problem solving, and have strong analytical skills. They should work well under stress and communicate well with users from a range of technical backgrounds. Working in a field that changes rapidly, they should be enthusiastic about learning new technologies as they are developed.

EXPLORING

If you are interested in this field, think about organizing a career day with an employed technical support specialist. Local computer repair shops that offer technical support services are a good place to look. Otherwise, you could contact major corporations, computer companies, and even the central office of your school system.

If you are interested in any computer field, you should start working and playing on computers as much as possible. You can surf the Internet, read computer magazines, and join a school or community computer club. You might also attend a computer technology course at a local technical/vocational school.

◆ RESOURCES

Association for Computing Machinery
One Astor Plaza
1515 Broadway
New York, NY 10036
Tel: 212-869-7440
Web: http://www.acm.org

IEEE Computer Society
1730 Massachusetts Avenue, NW
Washington, DC 20036-1992
Tel: 202-371-0101
Web: http://www.computer.org

CHAPTER 4

Environmental Activities

> **"** *We like to see involvement in school, community, church activities—reaching outside oneself to do something for others.* **"**
>
> *– Chuck Morgan, Associate Director of Admission,*
> *Berea College, Berea, Kentucky*

✦ INTRODUCTION

The environment encompasses everything from the earth we walk on to the air we breathe—and talk of both its demise and efforts to preserve it has become increasingly common.

Do you find your ears perking up when you hear a news report on a battle over logging in the Pacific Northwest? Do you feel vindicated after watching movies like *Erin Brockovich?* Perhaps you enjoy long walks through the woods or marvel at the magnificence of the endangered humpback whale.

Studying plant and animal habitats, documenting the phenomena that affect our daily lives, and working to protect and conserve our natural resources are all aspects of the important careers that relate to the environment.

Only a small percentage of the jobs in this field are represented in this chapter, but in reading about them, you may discover that a "green" career is for you.

ECOLOGISTS

✦ OVERVIEW

Ecology is the study of the interconnections between organisms (plants, animals) and the physical environment. It links biology, which includes both zoology and botany, with physical sciences such as geology and paleontology. Thus, *ecologist* is a broad name for any of a number of different biological or physical scientists concerned with the study of plants or animals within their environment.

The main unit of study in ecology is the ecosystem. Ecosystems are communities of plants and animals within a given habitat that provide the necessary means of survival, including food and water. Examples include forests, tundra, savannas (grasslands), and rain forests. Ecosystems are defined by such physical conditions as climate, altitude, latitude, and soil and water characteristics.

A primary concern of ecologists today is preserving ecosystems against the threats of pollution, overuse of land, and other dangers. A growing area of expertise is the reconstruction of ecosystems that have been destroyed or nearly destroyed by these environmental abuses.

✦ EARNINGS

According to the Ecological Society of America, salaries for ecologists can range from $10,000 per year to $175,000 and above. Salaries of $175,000 or more are quite rare, however. Most experienced and successful ecologists in academia and government can hope to earn salaries of no more than $85,000. The median income for ecologists is about $45,000. Federal agency jobs tend to pay more than state or local agency jobs. Private-sector jobs typically pay more than public-sector jobs.

✦ OUTLOOK

Environmentally oriented jobs are expected to increase at a faster rate than the average for all occupations through 2008, according to the US Department of Labor. Land and resource conservation jobs tend to be the most scarce, however, because of high popularity and tight budgets for agencies. Those with advanced degrees will fare better than ecologists with only bachelor's degrees.

✦ TRAINING

A bachelor of science degree is the minimum degree required for nonresearch jobs in ecology, which include testing and inspection. A master's degree is necessary for jobs in applied research or management. A PhD is generally required to advance in the field, including into administrative positions.

The Environmental Careers Organization (ECO) says that if you can only take one undergraduate major, it should be in the basic sciences: biology, botany, zoology, chemistry, physics, or geology. ECO adds that at the master's degree level, natural resource management, ecology, botany, conservation biology, and forestry studies are useful.

Ecologists should appreciate and respect nature, be well versed in scientific fundamentals, and be able to work and communicate well with other people.

✦ EXPLORING

You can seek more information about ecology from guidance counselors and professional ecologists at nearby colleges, universities, and government agencies. An easy way for you to learn more about ecology is to study your own environment. Trips to a nearby pond, forest, or park over the course of several months will provide opportunities to observe and collect data. Science teachers and local park service or arboretum personnel can also offer you guidance.

✦ RESOURCES

Ecological Society of America
2010 Massachusetts Avenue, NW, Suite 400
Washington, DC 20036
Tel: 202-833-8773
Web: http://www.sdsc.edu/projects/ESA/esa.htm

National Wildlife Federation
8925 Leesburg Pike
Vienna, VA 22184
Tel: 703-790-4000
Web: http://www.nwf.org

Student Conservation Association
689 River Road
PO Box 550
Charlestown, NH 03603-0550
Tel: 603-543-1700
Web: http://www.sca-inc.org

ENVIRONMENTAL ENGINEERS

✦ OVERVIEW

Environmental engineers design, build, and maintain systems to control wastewater, solid waste, hazardous waste, and contaminated emissions produced by municipalities or private industry. Environmental engineers are typically employed by the Environmental Protection Agency (EPA), private industry, or engineering consulting firms.

Broadly speaking, environmental engineers may focus on one of three areas: air, land, or water. A big area for environmental engineers is hazardous waste management. Expertise in designing systems and processes to reduce, recycle, and treat hazardous waste streams is very much in demand. This area tends to be the most technical of all the environmental fields and demands professionals with graduate and technical degrees.

Environmental engineers spend a lot of time on paperwork, including writing reports and memos and filling out forms. On a given day, an environmental engineer might be found climbing a smokestack, wading in a creek, or going toe-to-toe with a district attorney in a battle over a compliance matter.

✦ EARNINGS

According to the Environmental Careers Organization (ECO), average solid waste management pay is slightly lower than that for hazardous waste management. Entry-level salaries for professionals in this field range from less than $20,000 to $30,000, with engineers at the higher end of the scale. In water quality management, starting pay ranges from about $30,000 to $40,000 for state and federal government jobs. For private jobs, pay starts at about $30,000.

✦ OUTLOOK

The environmental engineering job market has tapered off from its rapid growth in the 1980s, when increased environmental regulations forced states to clean up hazardous waste sites and the EPA required companies to reduce waste and dispose of it more responsibly.

Overall, the water supply and water pollution control specialties currently offer the most job opportunities for environmental engineers. Opportunities are available with all three major employers—the EPA, private industry, and consulting firms, with the latter two offering the best possibilities.

✦ TRAINING

A bachelor's degree is mandatory to work in environmental engineering. About 20 schools offer an undergraduate degree in environmental engineering. Other possibilities are to earn a traditional engineering degree with an environmental focus, to obtain a traditional engineering degree and pick up the environmental knowledge on the job, or to earn a masters' degree in environmental engineering.

If your work as an engineer affects public health, safety, or property, you must register with the state. To obtain registration, you must have a degree from an accredited engineering program and pass an exam.

This field calls for resourceful people who like solving problems and have a solid background in science and math. You should also enjoy being outdoors and have a strong desire to protect the environment.

EXPLORING

A good way to explore becoming an environmental engineer is to talk to someone in the field. Contact your local EPA office, check the phone book for environmental consulting firms in your area, or ask a local industrial company if you can visit. The latter is not as far-fetched as you might think: big industry has learned the value of building positive community relations, and their outreach efforts may include having an open house in which one can walk through their plants, ask questions, and get a feel for what goes on there.

You also might volunteer for the local chapter of a nonprofit environmental organization, do an internship through ECO or another organization, or work first as an environmental technician, a job that requires less education (such as a two-year associate degree or even a high school diploma).

RESOURCES

American Academy of Environmental Engineers
130 Holiday Court, Suite 100
Annapolis, MD 21401
Tel: 410-266-3311
Web: http://www.enviro-engrs.org

National Association of Environmental Professionals
6524 Ramoth Drive
Jacksonville, FL 32226-3202
Tel: 904-251-9900
Web: http://www.naep.org

National Solid Wastes Management Association
4301 Connecticut Avenue, NW, Suite 300
Washington, DC 20008
Tel: 202-244-4700
Web: http://www.envasns.org/nswma

Student Conservation Association
689 River Road
PO Box 550
Charlestown, NH 03603-0550
Tel: 603-543-1700
Web: http://www.sca-inc.org

ENVIRONMENTAL LOBBYISTS

✦ OVERVIEW

Like other lobbyists, *environmental lobbyists* strive to influence legislation on behalf of a client or special interest group. Environmental lobbyists, however, deal specifically with environmental issues. They urge legislators and other government officials to support measures that will protect endangered species, limit the exploitation of natural resources, impose stricter antipollution regulations, and impose other conservation measures.

Environmental lobbyists meet with members of Congress, their staff members, and other members of government. They sometimes testify before congressional committees or state legislatures as well as distribute letters and fact sheets to legislators' offices.

Indirect lobbying, also called grassroots lobbying, involves educating and motivating the public and encouraging citizens to influence their representatives to vote for or against certain legislation. This is done through press releases, letters, and even going door to door.

✦ EARNINGS

Environmental lobbyists usually work for not-for-profit organizations with extremely limited budgets. Consequently, their salaries tend to be much lower than those of other lobbyists. While most lobbyists may earn anywhere from $12,000 to $700,000, depending on the groups they represent and their years of experience, environmental lobbyists are more likely to earn between $12,000 and $80,000.

✦ OUTLOOK

Regrettably, there is no shortage of environmental concerns in our country. As long as people continue to pollute our air and water, cut down forests, develop land, and mine the earth, environmental groups will continue to fight for legislation that will protect our natural resources. This profession is, therefore, expected to grow about as fast as the average through 2008.

The nation's economy can affect environmental protection organizations, which are largely funded by donations. During recessions, people may not be able to give as generously to not-for-profit organizations—something to consider for the long term. And despite recent economic growth in the United States, a proliferation of nonprofits has increased the competition for funding sources.

TRAINING

While there are no specific educational requirements for environmental lobbyists, most have college degrees; a growing number also have advanced degrees. Recommended courses are those that will help you understand the complex issues behind legislation: environmental science, geography, economics, political science, and history. Lobbyists must be able to do more than understand the issues, however—they must also be able to write and speak about them in a convincing manner. Courses in communications, public relations, and English can all be helpful.

Environmental lobbyists must be tenacious, self-motivated, able to work well with others, and perform effectively under pressure. They must have a solid understanding of the political process and feel confident approaching government officials and powerful legislators. Most important, they must be committed to protecting the environment.

EXPLORING

To explore this field, consider serving as an intern for an environmental organization. Internships can help you gain hands-on experience, learn about the issues, meet potential employers, and possibly even get college credit.

Political or government experience is also valuable for would-be lobbyists. Pursue a staff position within a legislator's office or seek out a government internship. Several agencies in Washington, DC, offer government internships, including the Library of Congress, the US Department of Agriculture, and the School of International Service at American University.

◆ RESOURCES

American League of Lobbyists
PO Box 30005
Alexandria, VA 22310
Web: http://www.alldc.org/

Environmental Careers Organization
179 South Street
Boston, MA 02111
Web: http://www.eco.org/

HAZARDOUS WASTE MANAGEMENT SPECIALISTS

◆ OVERVIEW

The title *hazardous waste management specialist* encompasses a group of people who do one or more of the following: identify hazardous waste; ensure its safe handling, cleanup, and disposal; and work to reduce generation of hazardous waste. Hazardous waste management specialists may work for a number of different employers, from producers of hazardous waste such as industry, hospitals, and utilities to government agencies who monitor these producers. They may also work for the solid waste or public health departments of local governments. Often they supervise hazardous waste management technicians, who do sampling, monitoring, and testing at suspect sites, for example.

◆ EARNINGS

Hazardous waste management specialists who enter the field with no experience earned around $30,000 per year in 1998; those who have experience as an intern or technician start at around $38,000, according to the *Princeton Review*. About three-quarters of all hazardous waste workers are employed by the private sector, with middle-range salaries averaging between $40,000 and $50,000 per year. Specialists with degrees in areas of high demand, such as toxicology or hydrology, can earn $80,000 or more, depending on seniority and certification levels. Specialists who obtained entry-level jobs with the government in 1998 earned starting pay between $19,969 and $24,734.

◆ OUTLOOK

The Environmental Careers Organization (ECO) calls hazardous waste management a "hot" environmental career. Hazardous waste management is currently suffering from a lack of qualified professionals; the sheer enormity of the hazardous waste problem, with over 40,000 known sites and more expected to be identified in the near future, ensures that there will be cleanup jobs available as long as funding is available. The mid-1990s saw a higher-than-average growth rate for hazardous waste management professionals, and that trend is expected to continue for at least the next decade.

ECO advises students to plan for changes in the field; whereas the current emphasis is on waste removal, neutralization, and disposal, future job markets will revolve around waste prevention.

TRAINING

Although some specialists enter this field with undergraduate degrees in engineering—environmental, chemical, or civil—an engineering degree is not strictly necessary for the work involved. Many employers in this field train their employees with the help of technical institutes or community colleges with courses on hazardous waste disposal. A bachelor's degree in environmental resource management, chemistry, geology, or ecology also may be acceptable. To get work in the areas of hydrology or subsurface hydrology may require a master's or doctoral degree.

The relative newness of this field, its dependence on political support, the varied nature of its duties, and its changing regulations and technologies all require a large degree of flexibility from hazardous waste management specialists. The ability to take into consideration the many economic, environmental, legal, and social aspects of each project is key, as are thoroughness, patience, and excellent communication skills.

EXPLORING

Those who would like to explore avenues of hazardous waste management can get involved in local chapters of citizen watchdog groups and become familiar with nearby Superfund sites. What is being done at those sites? Who is responsible for the cleanup? What effect does the site have on its community?

There are numerous magazines published on hazardous waste management, and outreach programs sponsored by the US Army Corps of Engineers offer presentations to high schools in some areas. These can be arranged with the help of science departments and placement office staff.

◆ RESOURCES

Citizens Clearinghouse for Hazardous Waste
PO Box 6806
Falls Church, VA 22040
Tel: 703-237-2249
Web: http://www.essential.org/orgs/cchw

National Environmental Health Association
720 South Colorado Boulevard
Denver, CO 80222
Tel: 303-756-9090
Web: http://www.neha.org

National Partnership for Environmental Technology in Education

6601 Owens Drive, Suite 235
Pleasanton, CA 94588
Tel: 510-225-0668

US Army Corps of Engineers

Massachusetts Avenue, NW
Washington, DC 20314-1000
Tel: 202-761-0010
Web: http://www.usace.army.mil/

NATIONAL PARK SERVICE EMPLOYEES

◆ OVERVIEW

The National Park Service (NPS) employs thousands of people with a wide variety of backgrounds and responsibilities. *National Park Service employees* include *law enforcement* and *interpretive rangers, resource managers, historians, archaeologists, scientists, clerical assistants,* and *maintenance workers*—to name just a few. No matter what their responsibilities, these employees are all dedicated to the NPS's mission of conserving the natural and cultural resources of America's National Park System for the enjoyment, education, and inspiration of the present and future generations.

The NPS employees who probably have the most contact with visitors are park rangers. There are actually two distinct kinds of rangers: enforcement rangers, who enforce the rules and protect park resources, and interpretive rangers, who educate the public about park resources.

Scientists, historians, and archaeologists are behind-the-scenes workers, who study the cultural artifacts within our parks to help us better understand and manage the park's ecosystems.

The NPS also employs a limited number of museum professionals, who are involved in exhibit design, collection management, and museum education.

The employees and functions within each national park are all overseen by one individual. This person, called the *park superintendent,* is charged with making sure that our parks maintain the delicate balance between welcoming visitors and preserving natural resources. In larger parks, he or she may work with an *assistant superintendent.* In addition to supervising the various operations within the park, the superintendent handles land acquisitions, works with resource managers and park planners to direct development, and deals with local or national issues that may affect the future of the park.

◆ EARNINGS

The salaries for National Park Service employees are based on grade levels, which reflect their levels of responsibility and experience. The first level, called the General Schedule (GS), applies to professional, administrative, clerical, and technical employees and is fairly standard throughout the country. Firefighters and law enforcement are included in the General Schedule. The other, called the Wage Grade (WG), applies to employees who perform trades, crafts, or manual labor and is based on local pay scales.

Most rangers, for instance, begin at or below the GS-5 level, which, in 1998, translated to an annual salary of $21,370 to $27,778. The average ranger is generally at about the second step of the GS-7 level, which translates to a salary of $27,352. The most experienced rangers can earn $34,408, the highest salary step in the G-7 level.

To move beyond this level, most rangers must become supervisors, subdistrict rangers, district rangers, or division chiefs. At these higher levels, people can earn up to $70,000 per year. These positions are difficult to obtain, however, because the turnover rate for positions above the GS-7 level is exceptionally low.

◆ OUTLOOK

Although it covers a lot of ground, the National Park Service is really a very small government agency. Because the agency is small, job opportunities are limited and, although they are not highly lucrative, they are considered very desirable among individuals who love outdoor work and nature. Consequently, competition for National Park Service jobs is very intense. This is not a situation that is likely to improve, since turnover rates are low and new parks are seldom created. Students who are interested in working for NPS should not be discouraged, though. The National Park Service is always looking for dedicated people who are willing to work their way up.

◆ TRAINING

Although not currently required for all positions, prospective park employees should obtain a bachelor's degree. Most rangers currently in the park system are college graduates and many believe that this will soon become a requirement. Any individual who hopes to serve as a scientist, historian, or archaeologist within the parks must have a college degree, with a major in the relevant discipline. Those who plan to become rangers should place particular emphasis on science courses. Other recommended areas of study are history, public speaking, and business administration.

Because there is so much competition for National Park Service jobs—particularly ranger jobs—many candidates pursue additional training programs. Some, for example, undergo medical technician training or attend police academies. Others attend independent ranger academies to learn the fundamentals of law enforcement, emergency procedures, and fire-fighting.

National Park Service employees need to successfully combine two very different characteristics: They must have a keen appreciation for nature and also enjoy working with the public. They need to be friendly, confident, able to communicate clearly, and adaptable.

In addition to these general requirements, each of the positions within the National Park Service also involves a set of characteristics and abilities unique to that position. Superintendents, for instance, must be good administrators and have the vision to create long-term plans. Rangers must be able to react quickly and effectively in crisis situations and convey authority to individuals who are violating park rules. Interpretive rangers must have extensive knowledge about the resources in their parks and should be effective educators.

EXPLORING

Hands-on experience can be a distinct advantage when trying to enter this competitive field. Interested students can get this experience through the Volunteers in Parks program. As a volunteer, you might help park employees to answer phone calls, welcome visitors, maintain trails, build fences, paint buildings, or pick up litter.

Students who do not live near a national park should contact the Student Conservation Association (SCA), which provides volunteers to assist federal and state natural resource management agencies. The SCA brings together students from throughout the United States to serve as crew members within the national parks, living and working within the parks for four to five weeks at a time.

Volunteering to work in local or state parks on weekends or during the summer months will also give you a good idea of what this field is like.

RESOURCES

National Park Service
US Department of the Interior
1849 C Street, NW
Washington, DC 20240
Tel: 202-208-4648
Web: http://www.nps.gov/nps

National Parks and Conservation Association
1776 Massachusetts Avenue, NW
Washington, DC 20036
Tel: 202-223-6722
Web: http://www.npca.org/npca

National Recreation and Park Association
22377 Belmont Ridge Road
Ashburn, VA 20148-4510
Tel: 703-858-0784
Web: http://www.nrpa.org

Student Conservation Association

PO Box 550
Charlestown, NC 03603-0550
Tel: 603-543-1700
Web: http://www.sca-inc.org

RECYCLING COORDINATORS

◆ OVERVIEW

Recycling coordinators manage recycling programs for city, county, or state governments or large organizations like colleges or military bases. They work with waste haulers and material recovery facilities to arrange for collecting, sorting, and processing recyclables from households and businesses. In addition, they are often responsible for educating the public about the value of recycling and instructing residents on how to properly separate recyclables in their homes. A small percentage of their time is spent keeping records of recycling rates in their municipalities, helping to set recycling goals, and applying for state and federal funding to improve their programs.

◆ EARNINGS

Salaries vary widely for recycling coordinators. Starting salaries range from $22,000 per year in smaller counties or cities to $40,000 and higher for coordinators in larger municipalities, according to *The Complete Guide to Environmental Careers in the 21st Century,* a 1998 book by the Environmental Careers Organization (ECO). Another salary survey, conducted by the National Association of Counties in 1997, cited an average starting wage in counties with populations under 25,000 at $19,568. The average starting wage in counties with populations of 100,000 to 249,999 was $41,968. Some of the highest salaries reported were in counties with populations of over a million, including one where the starting wage was $60,507 in 1997.

◆ OUTLOOK

The outlook for municipal recycling coordinators is excellent. According to ECO, thousands of these professionals will be needed as more and more municipalities commit to full recycling programs and states strive to meet their increasingly ambitious waste-reduction and recycling goals. ECO says the job of municipal recycling coordinator is one of the fastest growing across all industries.

Nationwide, the waste management and recycling industries will need more people to run recovery facilities, design new recycling technologies, come up with new ways to use recyclables, and do related work. Private businesses are also expected to hire recycling coordinators to manage in-house programs.

Although the recycling industry is subject to business fluctuations, demand and new technologies have created a viable market for the recycled materials.

✦ TRAINING

Enthusiasm, an understanding of recycling issues, and business acumen have traditionally been more important in this field than any particular degree. This is still true to some extent, as colleges generally don't offer degrees in recycling coordination. However, a bachelor's degree in environmental studies or a related area is desirable. Some schools offer minors in integrated waste management. According to ECO, classes may include public policy, source reduction, transformation technology (composting/waste energy), and landfills.

Successful recycling coordinators have good communication and people skills for interacting with staff, contractors, government officials, and the public. Leadership, persuasiveness, and creativity are other characteristics they share.

✦ EXPLORING

If you are interested in exploring this career, you should start by getting familiar with the issues. Why are some materials recycled and not others? Where are the markets? What are some creative uses for recyclable materials? Explore what's going on both nationally and in your area. Get to know who's doing what and what the future needs are.

You could also tour a local material recovery facility and talk with staff there. You might even volunteer to work for a recycling organization. Communities often have groups that support recycling with fund drives and information campaigns. Municipal public meetings and workshops are also good places to learn about how you can help with recycling in your community.

✦ RESOURCES

Environmental Careers Organization
179 South Street
Boston, MA 02111
Tel: 617-426-4375
Web: http://www.eco.org

Environmental Industries Associations/National Solid Wastes Management Association
4301 Connecticut Avenue, NW
Washington, DC 20008
Tel: 202-244-4700
Web: http://www.envasns.org/nswma

National Recycling Coalition

1727 King Street, Suite 105
Alexandria, VA 22314
Tel: 703-683-9025
Web: http://www.earthsystems.org

CHAPTER 5

Language Clubs

Extracurricular activities help to promote personal growth, awareness, diversity sensitivity, leadership skills, and maturity.

– Robert Burns, Assistant Dean for Admissions,
Medical College of Ohio, Toledo, Ohio

✦ INTRODUCTION

World news coverage, global trade, the United Nations, international travel. What do jobs in these areas have in common? They all involve exposure to other languages. Most companies and organizations are realizing that doing business in this century is going to require working with other countries and communicating in languages other than English. Speaking and understanding a second language is becoming an increasingly valuable asset.

Does the prospect of working and interacting with people of different cultures and languages appeal to you? Think about how your skills and interests might fit into the jobs in this chapter. Some involve travel to exotic places. Some involve insightful thinking and reporting. Some involve diplomacy and a keen knowledge of history and economics.

Maybe one will be your passport to a lifelong career.

CUSTOMS OFFICIALS

OVERVIEW

Customs officials are federal workers who are employed by the United States Customs Service (an arm of the Treasury Department) to enforce laws governing imports and exports and to combat smuggling and revenue fraud. They make sure that people, as well as ships, planes, and trains—anything used to import or export cargo—comply with all entrance and clearance requirements at borders and ports.

Stationed in the United States and overseas at airports, seaports, and points along the Canadian and Mexican borders, customs officials examine, count, weigh, gauge, measure, and sample commercial and noncommercial cargoes entering and leaving the United States. It is their job to determine whether or not goods are admissible and, if so, how much tax, or duty, should be assessed on them. To prevent smuggling, fraud, and cargo theft, customs officials also check the individual baggage declarations of international travelers and oversee the unloading of all types of commercial shipments.

EARNINGS

Entry-level customs workers in the federal government earn between about $20,600 and about $25,500 per year. The average annual salary for customs officials is about $31,200. Supervisory positions earn beginning salaries from $37,744 to $45,236. Federal employees in cities where the cost of living is higher receive locality pay, which adds between 5.6 and 12 percent to their base salary. Certain customs officials are also entitled to receive Law Enforcement Availability Pay, which adds another 25 percent to their salaries.

✦ OUTLOOK

Employment as a customs official is steady work that is not affected by changes in the economy. With the increased emphasis on law enforcement, including the detection of illegally imported drugs and pornography and the prevention of exports of sensitive high-technology items, the prospects for employment in the US Customs Service are likely to grow and remain high.

✦ TRAINING

Applicants to the US Customs Service must have earned at least a high school diploma, but those with college degrees are preferred. Applicants are required to have three years of general work experience involving contact with the public or four years of college.

Applicants to the US Customs Service must be US citizens and at least 21 years of age. Like all federal employees, they must pass a physical examination and undergo a security check. They must also pass a federally administered standardized test. Although they receive extensive training, these agents need to have two years of specialized criminal investigative or comparable experience.

Customs officials must be in good physical condition, possess emotional and mental stability, and demonstrate the ability to correctly apply regulations and make clear, concise reports.

✦ EXPLORING

There are several ways for you to learn about careers with the US Customs Service. You can talk with people employed as customs inspectors, consult your high school career counselor, or contact local labor unions. Information on federal government jobs is available from offices of the state employment service, area offices of the US Office of Personnel Management, and Federal Job Information Centers throughout the country.

✦ RESOURCE

US Customs Service
Office of Human Resources
1300 Pennsylvania Avenue, NW
Washington, DC 20229
Tel: 202-927-2900
Web: http://www.customs.ustreas.gov

ESL TEACHERS

✦ OVERVIEW

ESL (English as a Second Language) teachers are educators who specialize in teaching the English language to people of all ages. Most students are immigrants and refugees, while some may be children of foreign-born parents who do not speak English. Classes focus on reading and writing and basic conversation and are often aimed at teaching students basic tasks, such as navigating public transportation, answering the telephone, and filling out a job application.

ESL teachers work in public and private schools, community centers, and churches and sometimes for companies and organizations.

✦ EARNINGS

While there are no specific salary reports for ESL teachers, the American Federation of Teachers reported that the average salary for US teachers in a 1997-98 salary survey was $39,347. The average salary for a beginning teacher with a bachelor's degree was $25,190. The average maximum salary for a teacher with a master's degree was $44,694. The Bureau of Labor Statistics reported that an English teachers' annual wage in 1997 was $43,840. Teachers are usually contracted to work nine months out of the year; some also teach summer sessions or do planning or administrative work.

✦ OUTLOOK

The US Department of Education predicts that one million new teachers will be needed by 2008. The demand for adult education teachers is also expected to grow faster than the average for all occupations through the year 2008, according to the Bureau of Labor Statistics.

If you specialize in ESL, you should have a promising future. According to the American Federation of Teacher's 1998 Salary Survey, school districts reported a considerable shortage of teachers of bilingual education. The growing immigrant and refugee populations in the United States should continue to increase the need for English language instruction.

✦ TRAINING

Teachers in public schools must be licensed under regulations established by the Department of Education of the state in which they teach. Not all states require licensure for teachers in private or parochial schools. There are about 500 accredited teacher education programs in the United States, most of which are designed to meet the requirements of their own state. Some states may require a master's degree. If a major in ESL is not available, students may major in education with a concentration in ESL.

ESL teachers need a great deal of patience and empathy, the ability to work well with students of all abilities and ages, and an interest in other countries and cultures.

◆ EXPLORING

Students interested in a career as an ESL teacher should get involved with people of different cultures through community service, school activities, or church programs. For example, you might volunteer to help with a refugee or immigrant assistance program. For firsthand perspective, speak to ESL teachers about the advantages and drawbacks of their job.

◆ RESOURCES

American Federation of Teachers
555 New Jersey Avenue, NW
Washington, DC 20001
Tel: 202-879-4400
Web: http://www.aft.org

National Education Association
1201 16th Street, NW
Washington, DC 20036
Tel: 202-833-4000
Web: http://www.nea.org

TESOL (Teachers of English to Speakers of Other Languages, Inc.)
700 South Washington Street, Suite 200
Alexandria, VA 22314
Tel: 703-836-0774
Web: http://www.tesol.edu

FLIGHT ATTENDANTS

✦ OVERVIEW

Flight attendants are responsible for the safety and comfort of airline passengers, from initial boarding to disembarkment. They are trained to respond to emergencies and passenger illnesses. Some of their other duties: instructing passengers on the use of emergency equipment; serving beverages and meals; and helping children, people with disabilities, and other passengers needing special assistance. Flight attendants are required on nearly all national and international commercial flights.

EARNINGS

Beginning flight attendants earned an average of $13,700 per year in 1998. Those with six years of flying experience earned an average of about $20,000, while some senior flight attendants earned up to $50,000 a year. Wage and work schedule requirements are established by union contract.

Flight attendants are limited to a specific number of flying hours. In general, they work approximately 80 hours of scheduled flying time and an additional 35 hours of ground duties each month. Flight attendants on international flights typically earn higher salaries than those on domestic flights.

Companies usually pay flight attendants' expenses—such as food, ground transportation, and overnight accommodations—while they are on duty or away from home base.

OUTLOOK

Employment opportunities for flight attendants are predicted to grow faster than average through the year 2008. To meet the growing needs of the traveling public, airline companies are using larger planes and adding more flights. Because federal regulations require at least one attendant on duty for every 50 passengers aboard a plane, this means there will be many more openings for flight attendants. On the down side, this field is highly competitive.

✦ TRAINING

Applicants with college-level education are often given preference in employment. Business training and experience in working with the public are also assets. The ability to speak a foreign language is helpful in jobs with international airlines.

Most large airline companies maintain their own training schools for flight attendants. Training programs typically last from four to six weeks and end with a series of practice flights, followed by an on-the-job probationary period (usually six months).

Flight attendants should be intelligent, poised, resourceful, and able to work in a congenial and tactful manner with the public. They also must have excellent health, good vision, and the ability to communicate clearly as well as the ability to respond quickly in emergency situations.

EXPLORING

Interested persons may explore this occupation by talking with flight attendants or people in airline personnel offices. Airline companies and private training schools publish brochures describing the work of flight attendants and send them out upon request.

RESOURCES

Air Transport Association of America
1301 Pennsylvania Avenue, NW
Washington, DC 20004
Web: http://www.air-transport.org/

Aviation Information Resources, Inc.
1001 Riverdale Court
Atlanta, GA 30337
Tel: 800-AIR-APPS
Web: http://www.airapps.com

Federal Aviation Administration
Web: http://www.faa.gov/

Flight Attendant Corporation of America
Web: http://www.flightattendantcorp.com/

FOREIGN CORRESPONDENTS

✦ OVERVIEW

Foreign correspondents report on news from countries outside of where their newspapers, radio or television networks, or wire services are located. Foreign correspondents sometimes work for a particular newspaper, but more often they work for wire services; today's media are more interested in local and national news and usually rely on wire services for their international coverage, rather than dispatching their own reporters to the scene. Typically only the biggest newspapers and television networks employ foreign correspondents. These reporters are usually stationed in one city but cover a wide territory and range of stories.

EARNINGS

Salaries vary greatly depending on the publication, network, or station as well as the cost of living and tax structure in the areas of the world where foreign correspondents work. Generally, salaries range from $50,000 to an average of about $75,000 to a peak of $100,000 or more. Some media will pay for living expenses, such as housing, education for a reporter's children, and a car.

✦ OUTLOOK

The employment outlook for foreign correspondents is expected to remain relatively stable. Although the cost of maintaining a foreign news bureau is high, and world news is of increasingly less interest to Americans than local and national news, the number of correspondents is not expected to decrease—there are simply too few as it is. In the near future, you can expect most job openings to arise from the need to replace correspondents who leave the job.

TRAINING

At least a bachelor's degree is needed to become a foreign correspondent. A journalism major is helpful but may not be essential. Other possible majors are political science, English literature, and communications. A broad educational background, including courses in economics and foreign languages, will serve you well.

To be a foreign correspondent, you must have a love of adventure, a curiosity about how other people live, diplomacy and tact, the courage to delve into controversial topics, the ability to communicate well, and the discipline to work individually. You also must be adaptable and flexible; the living conditions on some assignments can be primitive and isolating.

 EXPLORING

Experience in and exposure to the overall field of journalism may be gained by working on your school newspaper or yearbook. If you aspire to be a foreign correspondent, explore any opportunity you can to learn about other countries and cultures, including language classes, travel opportunities, and study-abroad programs. In college, students can do freelance writing or work as a "stringer"—writing stories and offering them to anyone who will buy them. Financially, this can be hard to do in the short run but can pay off substantially in the long run.

 RESOURCES

American Society of Journalists and Authors
1501 Broadway, Suite 302
New York, NY 10036
Tel: 212-997-0947
Web: http://www.asja.org/cw950615.htm

Association for Education in Journalism and Mass Communication
Lew Conte College, Room 121
Columbia, SC 29208-0251
Tel: 803-777-2005
Web: http://www.rwonline.com/orgnztns/olist/org-aejmc.html

Society of Professional Journalists
16 South Jackson
Greencastle, IN 46135-0077
Web: http://www.spj.org

FOREIGN SERVICE OFFICERS

◆ OVERVIEW

Foreign service officers represent the government and the people of the United States by conducting relations with foreign countries and international organizations. They work in Washington, DC, and in embassies and consulates throughout the world to promote and protect the United States' political, economic, and commercial interests overseas. They observe and analyze conditions and developments in foreign countries and report to the State Department and other agencies. They also guard the welfare of Americans abroad and help foreign nationals traveling to the United States. The work of foreign service officers is divided into four broad areas: administration, consular affairs, economic and commercial affairs, and political affairs.

◆ EARNINGS

Foreign service officers are paid on a sliding scale according to their qualifications and experience. In 1998, the approximate starting salary for new appointees without a bachelor's degree was $27,951 a year. Bachelor's and advanced degrees, along with knowledge of a foreign language, can earn you a greater salary at entry. Junior officers make up to $56,665 a year; career officers, between $47,619 and $94,927; and senior officers, from $99,200 to $118,400.

◆ OUTLOOK

This field is expected to grow about as fast as the average for all occupations in the near future, but competition for foreign service jobs is stiff. In recent years, the US international affairs budget has been drastically cut. Foreign aid funding dropped from 20 billion dollars in 1985 to 12.4 billion dollars in 1995. Seventeen US embassies and consulates were closed between 1991 and 1995. Funding being taken away from diplomacy is being spent on domestic concerns. This means that those people who are interested in protecting diplomacy and the strength of the Foreign Service need to closely follow relevant legislation as well as promote the importance of international affairs.

◆ TRAINING

Though the Foreign Service is open to any US citizen between the ages of 21 and 59 who passes the required examinations, you'll need at least a bachelor's degree to be competitive. Most foreign service officers also have graduate degrees. Candidates are expected to have a broad knowledge of foreign and domestic affairs as well as US history, government, economics, culture, literature, and business administration.

To be a successful foreign service officer, you must be intelligent, quick to learn, flexible, diplomatic, and adaptable to new cultures and traditions. You'll also need good people skills, the ability to work both independently and as part of a team, and good physical health.

 EXPLORING

As a member of a foreign language club at your school, you may have the opportunity to visit other countries. If such programs don't exist, check with your guidance counselor or school librarian about discounted foreign travel packages available to student groups. Also ask them about student exchange programs.

It may be difficult finding part-time or summer jobs that are directly related to foreign service, but check with federal, state, and local government agencies and local universities. Some schools use volunteers or part-time employees to lead tours for foreign exchange students.

 RESOURCES

American Foreign Service Association
2101 E Street, NW
Washington, DC 20037
Tel: 800-704-AFSA
Web: http://www.afsa.org

Foreign Service
US Department of State
PO Box 9317
Rosslyn Station
Arlington, VA 22219
Tel: 703-875-7490
Web: http://www.state.gov

INBOUND TOUR GUIDES

✦ OVERVIEW

Tour guides lead groups of people to sites of interest. Those leading short excursions to famous American destinations are called *inbound tour guides*. Inbound tours may last a few hours or several days. Tour guides handle pre-departure arrangements, including booking airline flights, ground transportation, hotels, and restaurants, as well as planning a group's entertainment and tour schedule. Inbound tour guides should be familiar with their locations, including being able to answer questions and provide interesting, educational commentary about various sites. They must also keep tabs on their groups' members, making sure they stay together and meet their itinerary.

✦ EARNINGS

The work of an inbound tour guide is often seasonal—extremely busy during the peak travel times of May through October and much slower in the off-season. Earnings can range from $9.75 to $20 per hour, not including tips. The 1997 US News Career Guide Online lists the average salary for an entry-level inbound tour guide as $20,000; average mid-level earnings, $35,000; and high end, $75,000. While traveling, guides receive their meals and accommodations free, as well as a daily stipend to cover additional expenses.

✦ OUTLOOK

This occupation should grow faster than average through the year 2008. In fact, the job of inbound tour guide was listed in a recent *US News & World Report* article on "20 Hot Career Jobs" for the future. Guides with both cultural and foreign-language skills, especially Russian, German, Spanish, and Japanese, will be in demand. The best opportunities in inbound tourism are in large cities with international airports and in areas with a large amount of tourist traffic.

✦ TRAINING

Although there is no formal educational requirement for becoming a tour guide, many guides do have some postsecondary training. Many two- and four-year colleges, as well as trade and professional schools, offer courses in tour management and guiding. Some large travel agencies offer their employees in-house training classes. Some tour guides, especially those who lead special interest tours, have bachelor's or master's degrees in particular subjects, such as art history or architecture.

In this profession, you must have good people skills, a take-charge attitude, strong leadership skills, the ability to deal with unforeseen difficulties and situations, patience, and a willingness to work long hours.

EXPLORING

You can explore this field and gain experience through a part-time or summer job as a tour guide. Local historical sites or museums often use part-time workers or volunteers to conduct tours. Also, take advantage of any opportunity you can to travel and learn about various sites and attractions.

◆ RESOURCES

National Tourism Foundation
546 East Main Street
PO Box 3071
Lexington, KY 40596-3071
Tel: 800-682-8886 or 606-226-4251
Web: http://www.ntaonline.com

Travel Industry Association of America
1100 New York Avenue, NW, Suite 450
Washington, DC 20005-3934
Tel: 202-408-8422
Web: http://www.tia.org

United States Tour Operators Association
342 Madison Avenue, Suite 1522
New York, NY 10173
Tel: 212-599-6599
Web: http://www.ustoa.com/

INTERPRETERS AND TRANSLATORS

OVERVIEW

Interpreters translate spoken passages of one language into a second language—for example, from English into Japanese. Many interpreters specialize in a specific subject matter, such as medicine or law. Other interpreters aid in communication between people who are unable to hear and those who can. There are two basic systems of interpretation—simultaneous, in which an interpreter converts sentences as they are being delivered, and consecutive, in which an interpreter waits until a speaker is finished with a sentence before converting it.

Translators focus on the conversion of written materials from one language to another—e.g., books and other publications, plays, technical and scientific papers, reports, speeches, and legal documents.

Interpreters and translators work primarily for the government and international companies and organizations. Often they are utilized for their cultural knowledge as well as their language expertise.

EARNINGS

Earnings for interpreters and translators can vary significantly. Interpreters working for the United States government earn from $19,700 to $55,000 a year to start. Jobs at the United Nations headquarters pay from $21,300 to more than $55,000 a year. Earnings are generally higher in private industry and at international agencies. While freelance conference interpreters might make $350 a day for State Department work, they can make $500 a day in the private sector. Most court interpreters work on a freelance basis, earning between $25,000 and $75,000 a year.

Fees charged by freelancer translators begin at $0.10 per word. By the hour, translators typically earn between $15 and $35, although many earn more than that. Trainee translators can expect to earn about $18,000 per year.

OUTLOOK

Employment opportunities for interpreters and translators are expected to grow about as fast as the average. However, competition for available positions will be fierce. With the explosion of new technologies, the economy is becoming increasingly global, causing a boom in overseas business travel. This has created a new demand for translators and interpreters. Other factors contributing to growth in this field are steadily rising rates of immigration and an increase in leisure travel, spurred in part by aging Baby Boomers.

◆ TRAINING

Because interpreters and translators need to be proficient in grammar, have an excellent vocabulary in each of the languages spoken, and have sound knowledge in a wide variety of subjects, most employers require college degrees. A number of educational institutions now provide programs and degrees in interpreting and translating. Scientific and professional interpreters often have graduate degrees in their field of specialty.

Translators and interpreters should be able to speak and read at least two languages fluently and be well-acquainted with the culture of the country or countries in which the languages are spoken. Interpreters must have good hearing, strong speaking skills, and a pleasant voice. Both interpreters and translators should have self-discipline and patience as well as a love of language.

◆ EXPLORING

If you have an opportunity to visit the United Nations, you can watch the proceedings to get some idea of the techniques and responsibilities of the job of interpreter. Learn another language and, if you have the opportunity, travel to the country where that language is spoken and hone your skills. You could also pick up a language and learn about another culture by regularly corresponding with a pen pal in another country. Become a member of a school club that focuses on a particular language, and join the school debate team to practice your general speaking skills.

◆ RESOURCES

American Association of Language Specialists
  1000 Connecticut Avenue, NW, Suite 9
  Washington, DC 20036
  Tel: 301-986-1542

American Society of Interpreters
  PO Box 9603
  Washington, DC 20016
  Tel: 703-883-0611

American Translators Association
  1800 Diagonal Road, Suite 220
  Alexandria, VA 22314
  Tel: 703-683-6100
  Web: http://www.atanet.org/

LIBRARIANS

✦ OVERVIEW

Librarians, who work in a variety of capacities, help people find information and resources for academic, professional, or personal use. They are needed wherever books, magazines, audiovisual materials, or other informational materials are catalogued and kept: in public, academic, and special libraries; school library media centers; corporations and associations; and government. A librarian's job can be broken down into three areas: user services, technical services, and administrative services.

A growing subfield is the job of information scientist. *Information scientists* design computer systems and procedures for collecting, organizing, interpreting, and classifying information via computer.

✦ EARNINGS

According to the *Occupational Outlook Handbook,* the average starting salary for a graduate with a master's degree from an accredited library school in 1996 was $28,700 per year. Librarians working in technical areas averaged $36,600, and reference librarians earned $45,000.

Special libraries offered an average starting salary of $31,915 a year in 1998, and with three to five years of experience, the salary increased to $40,000. Beginning medical librarians averaged $25,900 in 1995; all medical librarians earned an average of $40,800. In the federal government, the average salary was about $56,000.

✦ OUTLOOK

The employment of trained librarians is expected to grow more slowly than the average rate through the year 2008. Public libraries will be faced with escalating materials costs, tighter budgets, and increased circulation. Competition for jobs will be increasingly tight.

Employment opportunities will be best in special and research libraries, especially for those librarians with technical and scientific backgrounds. The outlook is also good for librarians skilled in developing computerized library systems, as well as for those with a strong command of foreign languages.

✦ TRAINING

To become a librarian, you will need a bachelor's degree—preferably from a liberal arts college that will give you a broad educational background—and a master's degree in library or library and information science. Special librarians, such as law or pharmaceutical librarians, must have a strong background in their area of specialty. For work in research libraries, university libraries, or special collections, a doctorate may be required. A doctorate is commonly required for the top administrative posts of these types of libraries, as well as for faculty positions in graduate schools of library science.

In many states, school librarians and library media specialists are required to earn teacher's certification, and public librarians must be certified in most states.

All librarians should have a love of obtaining and presenting information as well as the ability to master constantly changing technology. Other helpful attributes are strong interpersonal skills, patience, attention to detail, and good problem-solving capabilities.

✦ EXPLORING

There are several ways for you to explore this field, including what students already do: reading, doing research for class projects, and browsing through the school library. You can also talk with school and community librarians about their jobs. Join or even start your own library club. Pursue work as an assistant in the school library media center or a local public library. In college, you might be able to work as a technical or clerical assistant in one of your school's academic libraries.

✦ RESOURCES

American Library Association
Career Information
50 East Huron Street
Chicago, IL 60611
Tel: 800-545-2433
Web: http://www.ala.org/

American Society for Information Science
8720 Georgia Avenue, Suite 501
Silver Spring, MD 20910
Tel: 301-495-0900
Web: http://www.asis.org/

Canadian Library Association
200 Elgin Street, Suite 602
Ottawa, ON, K2P 1L5, Canada
Tel: 613-232-9625
Web: http://cla.amlibs.ca/

"*Extracurricular activities help to shape the total person.***"**

– Carol Hogan, Director of Admissions,
Embry-Riddle Aeronautical University, Daytona Beach, Florida

"*The role of extracurricular activities has become more and more important as part of a well-rounded liberal arts education. Students who have a broad based experience seem to be the most successful.***"**

– Dennis DePerro,
LeMoyne College, Syracuse, New York

CHAPTER 6

Music
Activities

*66Extracurricular activities are the icing on the cake. We need students
to be involved beyond the classroom. We need students who want to be
contributing members of a community. Extracurricular activities tell us
if we can expect that in our prospective students. 99*

– Jacqueline Murphy, Director of Admission,
Saint Michaels College, Colchester, Vermont

✦ INTRODUCTION

Music is a powerful and ubiquitous presence in our lives. We hear it in
movies, in stores and elevators, on the radio, and, of course, at concerts. From
Beethoven to the Beatles, Ella to Elvis, music is as diverse and wide-ranging as
the talent it takes to produce it.

There are many jobs in the music field that require skills and aptitudes
other than performing, playing, and singing. There are technical, organizational,
and business positions throughout the industry.

As you read this section, think about the kind of music you like as well as
your personal strengths. If you love to sing or have a special gift for playing an
instrument, you probably turned to this chapter first. But even if you don't consider yourself musically talented, there may be a career for you in this field.

Music could help your career hit a high note.

AUDIO RECORDING ENGINEERS

✦ OVERVIEW

Audio recording engineers oversee the technical end of recording. They operate the controls of the recording equipment—often under the direction of a music producer—in a studio during the production of music recordings; in film, television, and radio productions; and in other situations that call for sound recording. They monitor and operate electronic and computer consoles, making adjustments to achieve the desired results. They also solve technical problems as they occur during a recording session. They ensure that all equipment is in optimal working order and that the necessary equipment is on hand for a particular job.

✦ EARNINGS

According to The Recording Workshop, a school in Ohio that trains recording engineers, assistants to engineers in the music industry make from $12,000 to $18,000 a year to start. Experienced engineers earn salaries ranging from $18,000 to $50,000 a year. Audio engineers in the broadcast industry often earn higher salaries than those in the music industry. The National Association of Broadcasters and the Broadcast Cable Financial Management Association found that salaries for technicians ranged from $17,000 to $30,000 annually, while chief engineers averaged $38,000 a year. Those with considerable experience can earn as much as $91,000 a year.

✦ OUTLOOK

New technology is rapidly changing the way audio recording engineers do their jobs. More advanced computer systems and digital recording techniques are phasing out many of the responsibilities of entry-level technicians. The recording process has become faster and easier, allowing studio managers to book more sessions, which in turn may require a larger staff. Although this new technology is becoming more affordable, inspiring some performers to do their own recording, musicians will continue to seek out the expertise of studio professionals to take full advantage of digital and multimedia technology. Overall, this field is expected to experience little change or grow more slowly than the average.

✦ TRAINING

Although it is not a formal requirement, postsecondary training is becoming an essential step for becoming a successful recording engineer. Postsecondary education options include trade school programs and two- and four-year degree programs at universities. Universities incorporate music, music technology, and music business in a comprehensive curriculum that prepares their graduates to be highly competitive in the industry.

Being a recording engineer requires both technical skills and communication skills. Engineers must be patient, capable of working well with a variety of people, and have excellent leadership and troubleshooting skills.

 EXPLORING

Any experience you can get working in a music setting will provide excellent background for this field. You could take up an instrument in your school band or orchestra or perform with your own band. You might also have the opportunity to work behind the scenes with a music group or as a technician in a school sound recording studio or radio station. You can also write or call record companies or recording studios to get more information and interview working audio engineers for an insider's perspective.

 RESOURCES

Audio Engineering Society
60 East 42nd Street
New York, NY 10165-2520
Tel: 212-661-8528
Web: http://www.aes.org

Recording Industry Association of America
1330 Connecticut Avenue, NW, Suite 300
Washington, DC 20036
Tel: 202-775-0101
Web: http://www.riaa.com

Society of Professional Audio Recording Services
4300 Tenth Avenue North
Lake Worth, FL 33461-2313
Tel: 800-771-7727
Web: http://www.spars.com

COMPOSERS

✦ OVERVIEW

Composers create original music such as symphonies, concertos, and operas; scores for musical theater, television, and cinema; and music for popular recording artists and commercial advertising. They transcribe their ideas into musical notation using the elements of harmony, melody, counterpoint, and rhythm. Composers may create compositions out of sheer inspiration or they may be commissioned to write a piece of music for a particular purpose. Many composers now use computers in various aspects of their work.

✦ EARNINGS

A few composers make huge annual incomes, while many make little or nothing. Some make a very large income in one or two years and none in succeeding years. While many composers receive royalties on repeat performances of their work, most depend on commissions to support themselves. Commissions vary widely, depending on the medium, the size of the production, and other factors. According to a 1992 survey by Meet the Composer, commissions for concert music and jazz compositions ranged from $1,500 to more than $15,000; for theater companies, $3,000 to $12,000; for operas, $10,000 to $150,000; for film and television, $2,000 to $200,000; and for advertising, $300 to $50,000.

✦ OUTLOOK

The employment outlook for composers does not fluctuate greatly from year to year in the United States and is one field that does not respond to economic cycles of recession and prosperity. In the near future, it is expected to experience little change or grow more slowly than the average.

There are no reliable statistics on the number of people who make their living solely from composing; the general consensus is that very few people can sustain themselves through composing alone. The field is highly competitive and crowded with highly talented people trying to have their music published and played. There is a limited number of commissions available at any given time. On the other hand, many films continue to be made each year, and cable television companies are producing more and more original programs that call for the talent of composers.

◆ TRAINING

There is no specific course of training that leads one to become a composer. Many composers begin composing from a very early age and receive tutoring and training to encourage their talent. After high school, music students can continue their education at a college, university, or special music school or conservatory that offers bachelor's and advanced degrees. Most schools now offer related computer training as well as the traditional course of music study.

◆ EXPLORING

Musical programs offered by local schools, YMCAs, and community centers offer good beginning opportunities. It is especially helpful to learn to play a musical instrument, such as the piano, violin, or cello. Attending concerts and recitals and reading about music and musicians and their careers will also provide good background and experience. Young musicians can form or join musical groups and try writing music for the groups to perform.

◆ RESOURCES

American Composers Alliance
170 West 74th Street
New York, NY 10023
Tel: 212-362-8900

American Federation of Musicians of the United States and Canada
1501 Broadway, Suite 600
New York, NY 10036
Tel: 212-869-1330
Web: http://www.afm.org

American Society of Composers, Authors, and Publishers
One Lincoln Plaza
New York, NY 10023
Tel: 212-595-3050
Web: http://www.ascap.com

DISC JOCKEYS

OVERVIEW

Disc jockeys play recorded music and make announcements on radio shows and during parties, dances, and other special events. On the radio, they select and introduce music as well as present news, weather, advertising, and commentary of interest to their audience. Interviewing guests and making public service announcements may also be part of a disc jockey's work.

EARNINGS

The salary range for disc jockeys is extremely broad, with a low of $7,100 and a high of $102,676, depending on the size of the market and the station. The average salary in the late 1990s was $31,251, according to a survey conducted by the National Association of Broadcasters and the Broadcast Cable Financial Management Association.

OUTLOOK

According to the *Occupational Outlook Handbook,* employment of announcers is expected to decline slightly through 2008 due to the lack of growth of new radio stations. Due to this decline, competition will be great in an already competitive field.

While small stations will still hire beginners, on-air experience will be increasingly important. Knowledge of specific topics, such as business, consumer, or health issues, may give you an advantage over the competition.

TRAINING

Although there are no formal educational requirements for becoming a disc jockey, many large stations prefer applicants with some college education. Programs in telecommunications or broadcast journalism are two possible avenues to pursue.

Students interested in becoming a disc jockey and advancing to other broadcasting positions should attend a school that will train them to become announcers. There are some private broadcasting schools that offer good courses, but others are mediocre; students should get references from the school or the local Better Business Bureau before taking classes.

Union membership may be required for employment with large stations in major cities and is a necessity with networks. The largest talent union is the American Federation of Television and Radio Artists. Most small stations are nonunion.

 EXPLORING

If becoming a disc jockey sounds interesting, you might try to get a summer job at a radio station. Although you will probably not have an opportunity to broadcast, you can decide if that kind of work appeals to you.

Take advantage of any opportunity you get to speak or perform before an audience. High school activities such as debating and theater will help you learn good enunciation and projection.

Many high schools and colleges have radio stations on site where students can work as disc jockeys, production managers, or technicians. This experience can be a good starting point in learning more about the field. Some radio stations offer students financial assistance and on-the-job training in the form of internships and co-op work programs, as well as scholarships and fellowships.

 RESOURCES

Broadcast Education Association
1771 N Street, NW
Washington, DC 20036-2891
Tel: 202-429-5354
Web: http://www.beaweb.org

National Association of Broadcast Employees and Technicians
501 Third Street, NW, 8th Floor
Washington, DC 20001
Tel: 202-434-1254
Web: http://nabetcwa.org

National Association of Broadcasters
1771 N Street, NW
Washington, DC 20036-2891
Tel: 202-429-5300
Web: http://www.nab.org

MUSIC PRODUCERS

✦ OVERVIEW

Music producers are responsible for the overall production of commercially recorded music. They work closely with recording artists and audio recording engineers to produce profit-making recordings of the highest possible quality. They monitor and control the technical aspects of a recording session and see to the needs of the musicians and recording engineers. They also work on the final mixing and editing of a recording. Music producers are constantly seeking out new talent and project ideas. While reviewing prospective artists, they are also working to keep contracted artists happy. Their responsibilities often involve negotiating contracts and recording arrangements.

EARNINGS

It is difficult to cite an average salary for producers because they generally either make a lot of money or have a short tenure in the business. The income of a record producer is directly tied to record sales. An independent producer works on a royalty basis, which is whatever he or she can negotiate—usually from 3 to 5 percent of retail sales. They may also charge a fee or get an advance from the record company, which is then deducted from sales.

Starting out, producers often work as technicians for studios, making about $12,000 to $18,000 a year, according to The Recording Workshop, a school for the recording arts in Ohio. Producers working with leading performers can make well over $100,000 a year. The Mix 1998 Audio Production Facilities Report, compiled by *Mix Magazine,* lists the estimated median salaries of staff producers as $42,500 a year.

OUTLOOK

The recording industry is in a continual state of flux but is expected to grow about as fast as the average. New technology, new music, new markets, and new business methods are constantly redefining the job of music producer. Although employment for music producers is very competitive, projections for the industry are for continued steady expansion. New computer technology is simplifying the recording and mixing process while opening new outlets for creativity. Although some independent-label bands choose to produce themselves, major record labels will continue to rely on the experience and know-how of successful producers.

✦ TRAINING

After high school, you should seek postsecondary training in audio engineering. Seminars and workshops can teach you the basics of music recording. A trade school program will give you a more comprehensive understanding of the industry. The most complete level of postsecondary education is a two- or four-year degree from a university. Universities incorporate music, music technology, and music business in a curriculum that prepares their graduates to be highly competitive in the industry.

Music producers should have a good ear for music and the ability to get along well with others. They also need a great deal of insight into the history and current trends of the recording industry.

✦ EXPLORING

High school students can begin exploring this field by taking courses in music and learning to play an instrument. Learn about as many musical genres as you can. By joining a music group, you can get a sense of the collaborative process of putting songs together. Your school may also have equipment available for recording performances; your school's music teacher or media department director may be able to assist you in a recording project. Since a large part of being a producer involves good communication skills, any experience you can get dealing with a variety of people—as in a retail sales job, for example—will be helpful. Students can also contact record companies or recording studios to get more information.

✦ RESOURCES
National Academy of Recording Arts and Sciences
3402 Pico Boulevard
Santa Monica, CA 90405
Tel: 310-392-3777
Web: http://grammy.org
Recording Industry Association of America
1330 Connecticut Avenue, NW, Suite 300
Washington, DC 20036
Tel: 202-775-0101
Web: http://www.riaa.com
Society of Professional Audio Recording Services
4300 Tenth Avenue North
Lake Worth, FL 33461-2313
Tel: 800-771-7727
Web: http://www.spars.com

MUSICAL CONDUCTORS

✦ OVERVIEW

Musical conductors direct musical groups in performances, including symphony orchestras, dance bands, and choirs. They use their hands, a baton, or both to indicate the timing and musical sound variations of a composition. Their chief concern is interpreting how a piece of music should be played. Not only must they know the music, but they must be able to inspire the musicians they are leading.

Musical conductors are also responsible for choosing the music that is performed, directing rehearsals, and auditioning musicians. A conductor sometimes carries the title of musical director, which implies a wider area of responsibilities, including administrative and managerial duties.

✦ EARNINGS

The range of earnings for conductors is enormous. Many conductors work only part time and make small yearly incomes. Part-time choir directors for churches and temples, for instance, make from $3,500 to $25,000 per year, while full-time directors make from $15,000 to $40,000 per year. Conductors of dance bands make from $300 to $1,200 per week. Opera and choral group conductors make as little as $8,000 per year working part time at the community level, but salaries range to over $100,000 per year for those with permanent positions with established companies in major cities. A symphony orchestra conductor can make $25,000 to $40,000 per year conducting a smaller regional orchestra but can make $500,000 or more a year as the resident conductor of an internationally renowned orchestra.

✦ OUTLOOK

The competition for conductor jobs, already tight, will become even tighter in the next decade. The operating cost for an orchestra continues to grow every year, and musical organizations are in constant budget-trimming modes. This has tended to affect growth in the orchestra field and, accordingly, the number of conducting jobs. Additionally, the overall number of orchestras in the United States has grown only slightly in the last two decades. The number of orchestras in academia declined slightly, while community, youth, and city orchestras increased slightly. Overall, this field is expected to experience little change or grow more slowly than the average.

✦ TRAINING

Formal training in at least one musical instrument is necessary for future conductors. Keyboard instruction is particularly important. Some conductors become involved at the high school or college level leading a small group for whom they may also do some arranging and composing. Some institutions have developed formalized programs to teach the art of conducting. At universities without specific programs, interested students should take courses in composition, arranging, and orchestrating. Conductor training programs and apprenticeship programs are also available. Conductors need not only an extensive knowledge of music and musical history but also a strong general background in the arts and humanities.

Being a conductor requires a high degree of self-discipline, strong leadership skills, and a great deal of natural talent.

✦ EXPLORING

It is not possible to understand conducting beyond an elementary level without a good background in music. Students interested in conducting should go to as many musical performances as they can—symphonies, operas, musical theater—and study the conductors, noting their techniques and movements and how the audience responds. There are also many associations, reference books, and biographies that provide detailed information about conductors and their art.

✦ RESOURCES

American Federation of Musicians of the United States and Canada
1501 Broadway, Suite 600
New York, NY 10036
Tel: 212-869-1330
Web: http://www.afm.org

American Symphony Orchestra League
1156 15th Street, NW, Suite 800
Washington, DC 20005
Tel: 202-776-0212
Web: http://www.symphony.org

Conductors' Guild, Inc.
103 South High Street, Room 6
West Chester, PA 19382
Tel: 610-430-6010
Web: http://www.conductorsguild.org/

MUSICAL INSTRUMENT REPAIRERS AND TUNERS

 OVERVIEW

Musical instrument repairers and *tuners* work on a variety of instruments, operating inside music shops or repair shops to keep the pieces in tune and in proper condition. They usually specialize in a certain area, such as pianos and organs, band instruments, or stringed instruments. They are highly skilled crafts-people who have expertise in working with wood, metal, electronics, and other materials. According to the *Occupational Outlook Handbook (OOH)*, about two-thirds of all musical instrument repairers and tuners were self-employed in 1998; of the other half, 80 percent worked in music stores and the rest worked in repair shops or for manufacturers.

 EARNINGS

Full-time instrument repairers had a median income of about $23,010 in 1998, according to the *OOH*. The middle 50 percent earned between $17,780 and $29,500 per year, while those on the low end earned less than $13,230. The highest 10 percent earned nearly $39,000. Repairers and tuners who are self-employed earn more than those who work for stores or manufacturers, but their income is generally less stable. Repairers who gain an international reputation for the quality of their work earn the highest income in this field.

 OUTLOOK

Job opportunities for musical instrument repairers and tuners are expected to increase more slowly than average through 2008, according to the *OOH*. However, because training opportunities are limited, there is generally a greater demand for skilled repairers and tuners than there are people to fill openings. Individuals who are familiar with the trade or have taken classes in musical instrument repair technology will have more success in finding a job.

Another positive indicator is that the number of people employed as musicians is expected to increase. Because those instruments are costly, individuals, schools, and other organizations will be more likely to have them repaired than replaced.

TRAINING

The requirements for people entering the field of musical instrument repair vary according to the instrument. The minimal requirements are a high school diploma and a basic knowledge of music.

Most instrument repairers take many years to master their craft. Depending on the area of specialty, students work in instrument repair shops as trainees, take training courses at vocational schools and community colleges, or work under the supervision of experienced technicians.

Common requirements for all repairers include patience, attention to detail, manual dexterity, and a love of music and fine instruments.

 EXPLORING

Learning to play an instrument and obtaining a solid music background is the first step in exploring this career. High school and college music departments can be excellent sources of information. Interviews with and demonstrations by instrument tuners and repairers may be arranged through school vocational counselors, music teachers, or church music directors.

Part-time and summer jobs in repair shops may be difficult to obtain because full-time trainees usually handle the routine tasks of a helper. Nevertheless, it is worth applying for such work. Jobs in stores that sell musical instruments can also help familiarize students with the field and may offer the opportunity to observe skilled repairers at work.

◆ RESOURCES

Electronics Technicians Association
> 602 North Jackson Street
> Greencastle, IN 46135
> Tel: 765-653-8262

National Association of Professional Band Instrument Repair Technicians
> PO Box 51
> Normal, IL 61761
> Tel: 309-452-4257
> Web: http://www.napbirt.org

Piano Technicians Guild
> 3930 Washington
> Kansas City, MO 64111
> Tel: 816-753-7747
> Web: http://www.ptg.org

MUSICIANS

✦ OVERVIEW

Musicians perform, compose, conduct, and arrange music. Music performers include singers as well as instrumental musicians. Performing musicians may work alone or as part of a group, or ensemble. They may play before live audiences in clubs or auditoriums or they may perform on television or radio, in motion pictures, or in a recording studio. Musicians usually specialize in one type of music, such as classical, popular, country, jazz, or folk, but many musicians play several musical styles. Musicians practice constantly to perfect their techniques. Many musicians supplement their incomes through teaching.

EARNINGS

What you can earn in a music career is dependent upon your skill level, reputation, geographic location, type of music, and number of engagements per year. In major US symphony orchestras, musicians can earn from $22,000 to $90,000 annually. Popular musicians and instrumentalists are usually paid per performance—from $30 to $300 or more per night, on average. The most successful popular musicians, of course, can earn millions of dollars each year. For recording background music for film and television, the going rate is about $185 to $235 for a three-hour session. Church organists, choir directors, and soloists make an average of $40 to $100 each week, but this is often part-time work supplemented by other income. Music teachers in public elementary and secondary schools earned salaries in the mid-$20,000s in the late 1990s.

OUTLOOK

It is difficult to make a living solely as a musician, and this will continue because competition for jobs will be as intense as it has been in the past. Through 2008, the demand for musicians will be greatest in theaters, bands, and restaurants. The outlook is less favorable in churches and temples. The growing number of cable television networks and new television programs will likely increase opportunities for musicians. Digital recording technology has also made it easier and less expensive for musicians to produce and distribute their own recordings. The opportunities for careers in teaching music are expected to grow at an average rate in elementary schools and in colleges and universities but at a slower rate in secondary schools. The supply of musicians for virtually all types of music will continue to exceed the demand for the foreseeable future.

◆ TRAINING

Postsecondary study is not required to be a musician, particularly for those seeking a career in the popular music field. College or conservatory degrees are only required for those who plan to teach in institutions. However, it is a good idea for anyone going into music to acquire a degree. Scores of colleges and universities have excellent music schools, and there are numerous conservatories that offer degrees in music.

Musicians who want to teach in state elementary and high schools must be certified.

To become an accomplished musician requires an uncommon degree of dedication, self-discipline, and drive. But music is an art form, and musicians will succeed according to the amount of musical talent they have.

◆ EXPLORING

There are many opportunities for aspiring musicians to explore the field. Elementary schools, high schools, and institutions of higher education all offer avenues for musical training and performance, including choirs, bands, and orchestras. Music students taking private lessons can display their talents in recitals. There are numerous community amateur and semiprofessional theater groups throughout the United States that produce musical plays and operettas in which beginning musicians can gain experience. Churches and musical summer camps provide additional opportunities to practice and perform music.

◆ RESOURCES

American Federation of Musicians of the United States and Canada

1501 Broadway, Suite 600
New York, NY 10036
Tel: 212-869-1330
Web: http://www.afm.org

American Guild of Musical Artists

1727 Broadway
New York, NY 10019
Tel: 212-265-3687

National Association of Schools of Music

11250 Roger Bacon Drive, Suite 21
Reston, VA 20190
Tel: 703-437-0700
Web: http://www.arts-accredit.org/nasm/nasm.htm

SINGERS

✦ OVERVIEW

Singers perform music with their voices by using their knowledge of vocal sound and delivery, harmony, melody, and rhythm. They can be classified according to the music they perform, such as gospel, blues, rock, jazz, folk, classical, or country. Singers perform either as soloists or as members of a group, or ensemble. Members of a cappella groups sing without accompaniment. In opera, singers perform the various roles, much as actors, interpreting the drama with their voice. Classical singers are categorized according to their vocal range—soprano, contralto, tenor, baritone, or bass.

✦ EARNINGS

Competition in this field is high, and only a small percentage of those who aspire to be singers achieve glamorous jobs and multi-million-dollar contracts. Famous opera singers, for example earn $8,000 and more for each performance. Singers in an opera chorus earn between $600 and $800 per week. Classical soloists can receive between $2,000 and $3,000 per performance, while choristers may receive around $70 per performance. For rock singers, earnings can be far higher.

In general, average starting salaries are about $26,000, with some as low as $6,900 and some higher than $70,000. Singers on cruise ships generally earn between $750 and $2,000 per week, although these figures can vary considerably.

✦ OUTLOOK

According to the US Department of Labor, available jobs for singers, as for musicians in general, are expected to grow about as fast as the average in the next several years. The entertainment industry is expected to grow during the next decade, which will create jobs for singers and other performers. Because of the nature of this work, positions tend to be temporary and part-time. In fact, of all the members of the American Federation of Musicians, fewer than 2 percent work full time as singers.

✦ TRAINING

There are generally no formal educational requirements for those who wish to be singers. However, education and training are valuable, especially in younger years. Students who know early on that they are interested in a singing career are often advised to attend high schools that combine academics with intensive arts education in music, dance, and theater. Many find it beneficial to continue their study of music and voice in a liberal arts program at a college or university. Others attend schools of higher education that are focused specifically on music, such as the Juilliard School in New York. In addition, many singers are taught by private singing teachers and voice coaches, who help to develop and refine students' voices.

A love of music, natural talent, perseverance, and ambition are some of the traits of professional singers.

✦ EXPLORING

To explore this field, it is a good idea to listen to recordings and sing as often as possible. Join your church choir or a school choir or band. Seek out parts in school drama productions that involve musical numbers. Many high school students form their own bands and can gain experience performing before an audience and even being paid to perform at school parties and other social functions.

Some trade associations offer competitions and apprentice programs. Colleges and universities throughout the United States offer summer programs for high school students interested in singing and other performing arts.

✦ RESOURCES

American Federation of Musicians of the United States and Canada
>1501 Broadway, Suite 600
>New York, NY 10036
>Tel: 212-869-1330
>Web: http://www.afm.org

National Association of Schools of Music
>11250 Roger Bacon Drive, Suite 21
>Reston, VA 20190
>Tel: 703-437-0700
>Web: http://www.arts-accredit.org/nasm/nasm.htm

Opera America
>1156 15th Street, Suite 810
>Washington, DC 20005-1704
>Tel: 202-293-4466

SONGWRITERS

◆ OVERVIEW

Songwriters write the words and music for songs, including songs for recordings, advertising jingles, and theatrical performances. Songwriters may work alone or as part of a team in which one person concentrates on the lyrics while another person concentrates on the music. Many songwriters, of course, perform their own songs.

For most songwriters, writing a song is only the first part of their job. After that, they must work to produce and then sell their song to a record company, recording artist, film studio, or other prospective buyer.

◆ EARNINGS

Songwriters' earnings vary widely, from next to nothing to millions of dollars. A beginning songwriter may work for free or for low pay just to gain experience. A songwriter may sell a jingle to an advertising agency for $1,000 or thousands of dollars if their work is well known. Royalties from songwriting can range from $20,000 to $100,000 or more per year.

Those starting as assistants in music production companies or jingle houses may earn as little as $20,000 per year. Experienced songwriters at these companies may earn $50,000 per year or more.

◆ OUTLOOK

Most songwriters are unable to support themselves from their songwriting alone and must hold other jobs for supplemental income. The competition in this industry is extremely intense, and there are many more songwriters than paying projects. This situation is expected to continue into the next decade.

There are, however, a few bright spots for songwriters. The growth in independent filmmaking, cable television programming and advertising, and computer games and software featuring songs and music bodes well for songwriters. Another potential boom area is the World Wide Web. As more and more companies, organizations, and individuals set up multimedia Web sites, there may be an increased demand for songwriters to create songs and music for these sites.

◆ TRAINING

There are no specific requirements for entering the field of songwriting. All songwriters, however, will benefit from musical training, including musical theory, notation, history, and styles. As songwriting is an extremely competitive field, postsecondary education can only help you. Learning to play one or more instruments, such as the piano or guitar, will be especially helpful in writing songs.

On the technical side, you should be familiar with MIDI (musical instrument digital interface) and other computer technology, as these play important roles in composing, playing, and recording music today.

A creative imagination and the ability to invent melodies and combine melodies into a song are essential skills for a career in this field.

◆ EXPLORING

The simplest way to gain experience in songwriting is to learn to play a musical instrument and to experiment with creating your own songs. Joining a rock group is a way to practice writing music for several musicians. Most schools and communities have orchestras, bands, and choruses you can join. Working on a student-written musical show is ideal training for the future songwriter.

If you have your own computer, think about investing in software, an electronic keyboard, and other devices that will allow you to experiment with sounds, recording, and writing and composing your own songs. Your school's music department may have such equipment available.

◆ RESOURCES

Broadcast Music Inc.
320 West 57th Street
New York, NY 10019-3790
Tel: 212-586-2000
Web: http://www.bmi.com

National Academy of Songwriters
6255 Sunset Boulevard, Suite 1023
Hollywood, CA 90028
Tel: 800-826-7287
Web: http://www.nassong.org

National Association of Composers USA
PO Box 49256, Barrington Station
Los Angeles, CA 90049
Tel: 310-541-8213
Web: http://www.thebook.com/nacusa/index.html

*"Extracurricular activities are important
in the college admissions process.
Colleges take into consideration that students
are balancing activities with academics,
and it shows that students can adjust to many things."*

*– Kelly Stone, Associate Director of Admissions,
Sage Junior College of Albany, Albany, New York*

*"Extracurricular activities are very important
in giving us insight on the applicant's goals, aspirations,
and sometimes weaknesses. It allows us to fulfill
our mission of educating people for a lifetime of service."*

*– Scott Russell, Director of Admissions,
Antioch University, Marina del Rey, California*

CHAPTER 7

School
Publications

Schools are looking for well-rounded, involved students. Admitting this type of student improves the quality of campus life.

— Scott McIntyre, Assistant Director of Admissions,
Champlain College, Burlington, Vermont

✦ INTRODUCTION

Do you find yourself eagerly awaiting the morning newspaper to find out what transpired the day before? Do you love to write stories or lay out pages for your school yearbook? Perhaps you have a knack for photography. If so, you could be destined for a career in publishing.

The most high-profile jobs in this industry tend to be held by authors and newspaper columnists—names we read in the papers every day and see on shelves at the grocery store checkout. But there are opportunities in this field for just about anyone who is interested in publishing. And with the Internet playing a more prominent role in publishing today, the possibilities are growing.

Whether it's writing, editing, designing, or taking pictures, each career in this field is focused on communicating with an audience. Perhaps you will find a career that speaks to you.

ADVERTISING WORKERS

◆ OVERVIEW

Advertising is defined as mass communication paid for by a company or organization to persuade a particular segment of the public to adopt ideas or take actions of benefit to the advertiser. *Advertising workers* perform the various creative and business activities needed to take an advertisement from the research stage to creative concept, through production, and finally to its intended audience.

Advertising workers are employed at agencies, corporations, and service and supply houses. Their work is fast-paced, dynamic, and ever-changing. Today the advertising industry is influenced largely by Internet technology.

◆ EARNINGS

In advertising agencies, chief executives can earn from $80,000 to as much as $750,000 annually, while experienced account executives average $44,000 a year or more. Research directors average $61,000 annually, experienced analysts up to $51,800 per year, media directors between $46,000 and $92,400 annually, and media planners and buyers $27,500 to $32,500 per year. Advertising copywriters earn an average of $56,000 per year, art directors between $44,500 to $60,000 or more annually, and creative directors $92,000 per year. Production managers make about $31,000 per year.

◆ OUTLOOK

Employment opportunities in the advertising field are expected to increase about as fast as the average for all industries through the year 2008. Network television, cable, radio, newspapers, the Web, and other media will offer advertising workers an increasing number of employment opportunities. Other media, such as magazines, direct mail, and event marketing, are expected to provide fewer job opportunities. Advertising agencies will enjoy faster than average employment growth, as will industries that service ad agencies. Many nonindustrial companies will also be creating advertising positions. Competition for jobs, however, is expected to be keen because of the large number of qualified professionals in this traditionally desirable field.

◆ TRAINING

The American Association of Advertising Agencies notes that most agencies employing entry-level personnel prefer college graduates. Copywriters are best prepared with a college degree in English, journalism, or communications; research workers need college training in statistics, market research, and social studies; and most account executives have business or related degrees. Media positions are increasingly requiring a college degree in communications or a technology-related area. Media directors and research directors with a master's degree have a distinct advantage over those with only an undergraduate degree. Some research department heads even have doctorates.

Advertising workers must be able to interact well with others; communicate clearly; thrive in a fast-paced, changing environment; and be creative and imaginative. Knowledge of current computer technology is virtually a must.

◆ EXPLORING

For those aspiring to jobs in the advertising industry, insight can be gained by taking writing and art courses in school or through a private organization. A full- or part-time job at a department store or newspaper office also can be helpful. Some advertising agencies and research firms employ students to conduct market research or work as agency clerks or messengers. An internship at an advertising or marketing company is another way to explore the field as well as to determine your aptitude for advertising work.

◆ RESOURCES

American Advertising Federation
1101 Vermont Avenue, NW, Suite 500
Washington, DC 20005-6306
Tel: 202-898-0089
Web: http://www.aaf.org

American Association of Advertising Agencies
405 Lexington, 18th Floor
New York, NY 10174-1801
Tel: 212-682-2500
Web: http://www.aaaa.org/

American Marketing Association
250 South Wacker Drive, Suite 200
Chicago, IL 60606
Tel: 312-648-0536
Web: http://www.ama.org

ART DIRECTORS

◆ OVERVIEW

Art directors oversee all visual aspects of communication, from print to film to the World Wide Web. Art directors formulate concepts and supervise production in establishing corporate identities; advertising products and services; enhancing books, magazines, newsletters, and other publications; and creating the visual elements of television commercials, film and video productions, and Web sites. Art directors may specialize in such areas as packaging, exhibitions and displays, or the Internet.

Besides design and illustration, art directors must have at least minimal knowledge of photography, computers, writing, and production in order to supervise the work of their teams.

◆ EARNINGS

In general, art directors at advertising agencies earn about 10 percent more than their counterparts in general publishing. A beginning art director (most of whom already have experience in the field) can expect to make somewhere around $30,000 per year, with larger companies offering as much as $100,000.

According to *Advertising Age,* agencies that made less than $3.6 million in 1997 paid their art directors an average of $44,500, while agencies with gross incomes of $15 million to $45 million offered their directors average salaries of over $60,000.

◆ OUTLOOK

Since economic conditions in the late 1990s were favorable, employment in the general area of visual art is expected to grow faster than the average through the year 2008. Industries promising growth include retail, consumer products, publishing, film production, and multimedia communications.

On the other side of the coin, the supply of aspiring artists is expected to exceed the number of job openings. As a result, those entering the field will face keen competition.

◆ TRAINING

A college degree is usually a requirement for those interested in becoming art directors, but it is not strictly necessary. According to the American Institute of Graphic Arts, nine out of 10 artists have a college degree and almost two out of

10 have a master's degree. Besides two- and four-year colleges and universities, a number of professional art schools offer two-, three-, or four-year programs.

The work of an art director requires creativity, imagination, and attention to detail, as well as the ability to work well with other people and adhere to tight deadlines. Knowledge of computers is essential, as is an interest in current artistic trends and techniques.

◆ EXPLORING

High school students can get an idea of what an art director does by working on their school newspaper, magazine, or yearbook. Look for a part-time job at an advertising agency or assisting the advertising director of a newspaper.

There are a variety of advertising clubs around the nation that are open to students. In addition to keeping members up to date on industry trends, such clubs offer job information and other resources.

Developing your own artistic talent is also important. Practice on your own or take courses in painting, drawing, and other creative arts.

◆ RESOURCES

American Advertising Federation
1101 Vermont Avenue, NW, Suite 500
Washington, DC 20005-6306
Tel: 202-898-0089
Web: http://www.aaf.org

American Institute of Graphic Arts
164 Fifth Avenue
New York, NY 10010
Tel: 212-807-1990
Web: http://www.aiga.org/

Art Directors Club
250 Park Avenue South
New York, NY 10003
Tel: 212-674-0500
Web: http://www.adcny.org

Graphic Artists Guild
90 Johns Street, Suite 403
New York, NY 10038-3202
Tel: 212-791-3400
Web: http://www.gag.org

BOOK EDITORS

✦ OVERVIEW

Book editors plan the content of books and acquire and prepare the written material to be published. They may work on fiction books, gift books, trade books, textbooks, or technical or professional books, including reference works. A book editor's duties include evaluating manuscripts and accepting or rejecting them, rewriting, correcting spelling and grammar, researching and fact-checking, and overseeing production, including working with artists, designers, and printers. They also may hire reporters, writers, and editors; negotiate contracts with freelance writers; and plan budgets.

Book editors are employed at publishing houses, book packagers (companies that specialize in book production), associations, and government agencies.

✦ EARNINGS

A salary survey in the July 1998 issue of *Publishers Weekly* stated that editorial salaries were tied to the size of the publishing company. Salaries for entry-level jobs, such as editorial assistant, range from $25,000 to $45,000. Editors in more advanced positions earn from $52,000 to $53,800 annually. The annual salary for supervisory editors ranges from $43,300 to $88,700.

✦ OUTLOOK

Most editing jobs will continue to be competitive through the year 2008, and employment is expected to increase faster than average, according to the *Occupational Outlook Handbook*. The growth of online publishing will increase the need for editors who are Web experts. Turnover is relatively high in publishing—editors often advance by moving to another firm or by establishing a freelance business. There are many publishers and organizations that operate with a minimal salaried staff and hire freelance editors for everything from project management to proofreading and production.

✦ TRAINING

A college degree is a requirement for entry into the field of book editing. For general editing, a degree in English or journalism is particularly valuable, although most degrees in the liberal arts are acceptable. Degrees in other fields, such as the sciences, psychology, mathematics, or applied arts, can be useful in publishing houses that produce books related to those fields. Textbook and technical/professional book houses tend to seek out editors with strengths in specific subject areas.

Book editors need a sharp eye for detail and a compulsion for accuracy. Intellectual curiosity, self-motivation, and a respect for deadlines are other important characteristics. Knowledge of word processing and often desktop publishing is also necessary. Familiarity with Internet technology is helpful for prospective editors as well.

 EXPLORING

The best way to explore this field is to try your hand at writing, researching, interviewing, and production. Volunteer to work on your high school or college newspaper or yearbook staff. Many magazine and newspaper publishers and some book publishers offer internships for students. Working as an intern will give you direct exposure to the editorial and publishing processes.

◆ RESOURCES

Association of American Publishers
71 Fifth Avenue
New York, NY 10003-3004
Tel: 212-255-0200
Web: http://www.publishers.org

Editors' Association of Canada
35 Spadina Road
Toronto, ON, M5R 2S9 Canada
Tel: 416-975-1379
Web: http://www.editors.ca

Publishers Marketing Association
627 Aviation Way
Manhattan Beach, CA 90266
Tel: 310-372-2732
Web: http://www.pma-online.org/

COLUMNISTS

✦ OVERVIEW

Columnists write opinion pieces for publication in newspapers or magazines. Columnists can be generalists who write about whatever strikes them on any topic. Most columnists focus on a specialty, such as government, politics, local issues, health, humor, sports, or gossip. Some of their ideas are based on news stories and others on personal experience.

Some columnists work for syndicates—organizations that sell articles to many media at once. Most newspapers employ local columnists or run columns from syndicates. Some syndicated columnists work out of their homes or private offices.

✦ EARNINGS

Like reporters' salaries, the incomes of columnists vary greatly according to experience, newspaper size and location, and whether the columnist is under a union contract. But generally, columnists make higher salaries than reporters.

Average starting salaries for writers, including columnists, was about $20,000 in 1997, according to the Dow Jones Newspaper Fund. After several years of experience, columnists can make top salaries of $60,000 or more a year.

Freelancers may get paid by the column. Syndicates pay columnists 40 to 60 percent of the sales income generated by their columns or a flat fee if only one column is being sold.

✦ OUTLOOK

The number of newspaper reporter jobs is projected to decrease in coming years, but the number of magazine writer jobs is expected to increase. The number of columnists will likely remain fairly stable. If a newspaper is small, or falls on hard times, managing editors may expect a local columnist to also take on reporting duties.

Competition for newspaper jobs is stiff, and for columnist positions, even stiffer. It will likely be easier to find employment at smaller daily and weekly newspapers than at major metropolitan newspapers. Movement up the ladder to columnist is likely to be quicker, but the pay is less than at bigger papers. New publications on the Internet also may be good places to start.

✦ TRAINING

As is the case for other journalists, at least a bachelor's degree in journalism is usually required to be a columnist, although some have degrees in political science or English. Experience may be gained by writing for your college or university newspaper or through a summer internship at a newspaper or other publication. Try submitting opinion columns to local or national publications—the more published articles graduates can show to prospective employers, the better.

To be a columnist requires similar characteristics as for being a reporter: curiosity, a genuine interest in people, the ability to write clearly and succinctly, and the ability to thrive under deadline pressure. Columnists also need a certain wit and wisdom, the compunction to express strong opinions, and the ability to delve into controversial issues.

✦ EXPLORING

A good way to explore this career is to work for your school newspaper and perhaps write your own column. Participation in debate clubs will help you form opinions and express them clearly.

✦ RESOURCES

American Society of Journalists and Authors
1501 Broadway, Suite 302
New York, NY 10036
Tel: 212-997-0947
Web: http://www.asja.org/cw950615.htm

Association for Education in Journalism and Mass Communication
234 Outlet Pointe Boulevard
Columbia, SC 29210-5667
Tel: 803-798-0271
Web: http://www.aejmc.org

Society of Professional Journalists
16 South Jackson
Greencastle, IN 46135-0077
Tel: 765-653-3333
Web: http://www.spj.org

DESKTOP PUBLISHING SPECIALISTS

✦ OVERVIEW

Desktop publishing specialists use computerized page layout programs to prepare newsletters, brochures, books, and other documents for printing. They generally work under the supervision of a graphic designer on jobs that have already been conceptualized, but some do original design work as well. They typeset text, arrange and modify graphics, and create page layouts. After a document has been reviewed and approved, they prepare it for electronic transfer, either to be printed or published on the World Wide Web or a CD-ROM.

Desktop publishing specialists work for corporations, marketing and advertising agencies, service bureaus, and printing companies. Many work as freelancers.

✦ EARNINGS

There is limited salary information available for desktop publishing specialists, most likely because their duties can vary and often overlap with other jobs. According to a salary survey conducted by Printing Industries of America (PIA) in 1997, the average wage of desktop publishing specialists in prepress departments ranged from $11.72 to $14.65 an hour, with the highest rate at $40 an hour. Entry-level desktop publishing specialists with little or no experience generally earn minimum wage. According to the *Occupational Outlook Handbook (OOH),* full-time prepress workers in typesetting and composition earned a median wage of $421 a week, or $21,892 annually.

✦ OUTLOOK

The *OOH* projects the field of desktop publishing to be one of the fastest-growing occupations through the year 2008, increasing by about 75 percent. As technology advances, the ability to create and publish documents will become easier and faster, thus influencing more businesses to produce printed materials. According to a survey conducted by PIA in 1997, the electronic prepress segment of the printing market enjoyed the most growth, another positive indicator for the future of this field.

✦ TRAINING

Although a college degree is not a prerequisite, many desktop publishing specialists have at least a bachelor's degree. Many four-year colleges offer courses in technical communications and graphic design. Some two-year colleges and technical institutes offer programs in desktop publishing or related fields. Some professional printing and graphic arts organizations offer scholarship and grant opportunities.

Desktop publishing specialists are typically artistic and detail-oriented, have strong problem-solving skills, and can work well in high-pressure situations. They also must have a solid computer background.

◆ EXPLORING

Experimenting with graphic design and page layout programs on the computer will give you a good idea of whether desktop publishing is for you. If you subscribe to an Internet service, take advantage of any free Web space available to you and design your own home page. Join a computer club or volunteer to produce a newsletter or flyer for a local organization. Part-time or summer employment with a printing company or a company that has an in-house production or art department is a great way to gain experience and make valuable contacts.

◆ RESOURCES

Association for Suppliers of Printing, Publishing, and Converting Technologies

1899 Preston White Drive
Reston, VA 20191-4367
Tel: 703-264-7200
Web: http://www.npes.org

Desktop Publishers Journal

462 Boston Street
Topfield, MA 01983-1232
Tel: 978-887-7900
Web: http://www.dtpjournal.com

National Scholarship Trust Fund of the Graphic Arts

200 Deer Run Road
Sewickley, PA 15143-2600
Tel: 800-900-GATF
Web: http://www.gatf.org

ILLUSTRATORS

OVERVIEW

Illustrators create artwork for both commercial and fine art purposes. They use a variety of media—pencil, pen and ink, pastels, paints (oil, acrylic, and watercolor), airbrush, collage, and computer technology. Illustrations are used to decorate, describe, inform, clarify, instruct, and attract attention. They appear everywhere in print and electronic formats, including television commercials, children's and other books, magazines, newspapers, signs and billboards, packaging, Web sites, computer programs, greeting cards, calendars, stationery, and direct mail.

Illustrators who are not self-employed work in advertising agencies, design firms, commercial art and reproduction firms, and printing and publishing firms. They are also employed in the motion picture and television industries, wholesale and retail trade establishments, and public relations firms.

EARNINGS

The pay for illustrations can be as little as a byline, though in the beginning of an illustrator's career, a job may be worth that just to get exposure. Some illustrators earn several thousand dollars for a single work. Freelance work is often insecure because of the fluctuation in pay rates and steadiness of work. Median earnings for salaried visual artists, who usually work full-time, were about $31,690 a year in 1998. The middle 50 percent earned between $23,790 and $41,980 a year. The top 10 percent earned more than $64,580, and the bottom 10 percent earned less than $18,000.

✦ OUTLOOK

Employment of visual artists is expected to grow faster than the average for all occupations through the year 2008, according to the *Occupational Outlook Handbook*. The growth of the Internet should provide opportunities for illustrators, although this might be tempered by the increased use of computer-aided design systems, which do not necessarily call for artistic talent or training.

✦ TRAINING

Talent is perhaps more important to an illustrator's success than education. Education, however, opens doors to new techniques, media, and ideas and helps beginning illustrators build a portfolio. To find a salaried position as an illustrator, you will need at least a high school diploma and preferably an associate degree in commercial art or fine art. The *Occupational Outlook Handbook* says nine out of 10 visual artists have a college degree. Whether you are looking for a full-time employment or freelance assignments, you will need a portfolio that contains samples of your best work. Employers are most interested in work that has been published or printed.

◆ EXPLORING

If you feel you are artistic and able to draw well, gain as much drawing experience as you can. Practice as much as possible on your own, drawing people, places, and objects from different perspectives. Take classes in school or through a community center or art school. Use any opportunity you can to present your work—for example, you could volunteer to do illustrations for your school newspaper or yearbook. You can also enter local art contests. Finally, seek out people currently working as illustrators and talk to them about the field.

◆ RESOURCES

American Institute of Graphic Arts
164 Fifth Avenue
New York, NY 10010
Tel: 212-807-1990
Web: http://www.aiga.org/

Society of Children's Book Writers and Illustrators
22736 Vanowen Street, Suite 106
West Hills, CA 91307
Tel: 818-888-8760
Web: http://www.scbwi.org/

Society of Illustrators
128 East 63rd Street
New York, NY 10021-7392
Tel: 212-838-2560
Web: http://www.societyillustrators.org

LITERARY AGENTS

✦ OVERVIEW

Literary agents serve as intermediaries between writers and potential buyers of their work, including publishers, editors, and movie and television producers. They also represent actors, artists, athletes, musicians, politicians, and other public figures who may seek to undertake writing endeavors. In essence, they sell their clients' creative talent. In addition to marketing their clients' manuscripts, literary agents also may negotiate contracts, pursue publicity, and advise clients in their careers.

✦ EARNINGS

In the late 1990s, agents generally earned between $20,000 and $60,000 annually, with a few making hundreds of thousands of dollars a year. Because independent agents take a percentage of their clients' earnings (4 to 20 percent), their livelihoods are contingent upon the success of their clients, which is, in turn, contingent on the agents' promotional abilities. Beginning agents can go as long as a year without making any money at all, but, if at the end of that time, their clients begin to gain notice, the agents' investment of time may well pay off.

According to the Association of Authors' Representatives, New York agency assistants typically earn beginning salaries of about $20,000. Sometimes agency staffers working on commission actually can earn more money than their bosses.

✦ OUTLOOK

Agents work in an extremely competitive field. Most agents who attempt to go into business for themselves fail within one year. Most job openings within agencies are the result of turnover, rather than the development of new positions. There are many candidates for few positions.

✦ TRAINING

A college degree is not necessary, but would-be agents with a college degree are more likely to be hired than those without. Recommended areas of study include liberal arts, performing arts, and business administration. It is also helpful to study law, although agents do not need to be lawyers.

Agents must have a knack for recognizing and promoting marketable talent. You must be familiar with the needs of publishers so as to approach them with appropriate and timely manuscripts. You also must be persistent, flexible, able to establish new relationships quickly, and able to interact tactfully and amicably with a wide variety of people, from demanding clients to busy editors.

◆ EXPLORING

If you are interested in literary management, you can acquaint yourself with current trends in book publishing and different publishing houses by working part time at a book store or library. You also may be able to get a job or internship with a book or magazine publisher, especially if you live in a big city. Some literary agents sponsor internships as well.

◆ RESOURCE

Association of Authors' Representatives, Inc.
PO Box 237201
Ansonia Station
New York, NY 10003
Tel: 212-353-3709
Web: http://www.publishersweekly.com/aar/

MAGAZINE EDITORS

◆ OVERVIEW

Magazine editors plan the contents of a magazine, assign articles, select photographs and artwork to enhance the articles, and edit or rewrite the articles. The editor also sets a budget and negotiates contracts with freelance writers, photographers, and artists. Most magazines focus on a particular topic, such as news, fashion, or sports. The editor must know the latest trends in the field the magazine represents. Depending on the magazine's size, editors may specialize in a particular area. For example, a fashion magazine may have a beauty editor, features editor, short story editor, and fashion editor.

EARNINGS

In the late 1990s, annual salaries for editorial assistants ranged from $20,000 to $28,000; experienced editors, $25,000 to $43,000; and supervisory editors, $33,000 to $57,200. Senior editors at large-circulation magazines averaged more than $75,000 a year. Many editors supplement their salaried income by doing freelance work.

◆ OUTLOOK

Magazine publishing is a dynamic industry. New magazines are continually launched, although many fail. A recent trend in magazine publishing is focus on a special interest. There is increasing opportunity for employment at special interest and trade magazines for those whose backgrounds complement a magazine's specialty. Association magazines, according to *Jobs '97,* offer good employment opportunities. Magazine editing is keenly competitive, however, and as with any career, the applicant with the most education and experience usually has the advantage.

TRAINING

A college degree is required for entry into this field. A degree in journalism, English, or communications is the most standard degree for a magazine editor. Specialized publications prefer a degree in the magazine's specialty—such as chemistry for a chemistry magazine—as well as experience in writing and editing. A broad liberal arts background is important for work at any magazine.

Magazine editors must have good judgment and a superior command of language, grammar, punctuation, and spelling. They also must be deadline-oriented and have a solid grasp of word processing and desktop publishing programs.

✦ EXPLORING

The best way to explore this field is to try your hand at writing, researching, interviewing, and production. Volunteer to work on your high school or college newspaper or yearbook staff. Many magazine and newspaper publishers offer internships for students. Working as an intern will give you direct exposure to the editorial and publishing processes as well as contacts in the field.

✦ RESOURCES

Association for Education in Journalism and Mass Communication
234 Outlet Pointe Boulevard
Columbia, SC 29210-5667
Tel: 803-798-0271
Web: http://www.aejmc.org

Editors' Association of Canada
35 Spadina Road
Toronto, ON, M5R 2S9, Canada
Tel: 416-975-1379
Web: http://www.editors.ca

Magazine Publishers of America
919 Third Avenue, 22nd Floor
New York, NY 10022
Tel: 212-872-3700
Web: http://www.magazine.org

NEWSPAPER EDITORS

OVERVIEW

Newspaper editors assign, review, edit, rewrite, and sometimes lay out copy for a newspaper. Editors sometimes write stories or editorials that offer opinions on issues. They review the editorial page and copy written by staff or syndicated columnists. They also check wire services for late-breaking stories. A large metropolitan daily newspaper staff includes various editors, each in charge of a specific area—sports, business, or city news, for example. A small weekly paper, on the other hand, may have only one editor, who might be both owner and star reporter. Today's newspaper editors depend heavily on computers, often working off site and submitting copy via modem.

Once an article is completed, *newspaper copy editors* correct spelling, grammar, and punctuation; edit for clarification; and check for factual accuracy. Copy editors sometimes write headlines and photo captions as well.

EARNINGS

Newspaper editors' salaries depend largely on the extent of their education and previous experience, their job level, and the newspaper's circulation. Large metropolitan dailies offer higher paying jobs, while small weekly papers pay less. According to the *Occupational Outlook Handbook (OOH),* beginning writers and editorial assistants averaged $21,000 annually, while those with five or more years of experience earned more than $30,000. Senior editors at large newspapers earned more than $67,000 annually. Salary ranges and benefits for nonmanagerial editorial workers on many newspapers are negotiated by the Newspaper Guild.

✦ OUTLOOK

Despite the competitive nature of this field, employment of newspaper editors and writers should be faster than the average through 2008, according to the *OOH*. Opportunities will be better on small daily and weekly newspapers. Some publications hire freelance editors to support reduced full-time staffs. And as experienced editors leave the workforce or move to other fields, job openings will occur.

✦ TRAINING

A college degree is required for entry into this field. According to *Jobs '97,* nearly 85 percent of first-time journalists had journalism or mass communications degrees. Journalism courses include reporting, writing, and editing; press law and ethics; journalism history; graphics; and photojournalism. Some schools offer internships for credit.

Newspapers look closely at extracurricular activities, emphasizing internships, school newspaper and freelance writing and editing, and part-time newspaper work. Computer skills are necessary and a knowledge of printing is helpful.

◆ EXPLORING

The best way to explore this field is to try your hand at writing, researching, interviewing, and production. Volunteer to work on your high school or college newspaper or yearbook staff. Many newspaper publishers offer internships for students. Working as an intern will give you direct exposure to the editorial and publishing processes.

◆ RESOURCES

American Society of Newspaper Editors
11690B Sunrise Valley Drive
Reston, VA 20191-1409
Tel: 703-453-1122
Web: http://www.asne.org

Dow Jones Newspaper Fund
PO Box 300
Princeton, NJ 08543-0300
Tel: 609-452-2820
Web: http://www.dj.com/newsfund

National Newspaper Publishers Association
3200 13th Street, NW
Washington, DC 20010
Tel: 202-588-8764
Web: http://www.nnpa.org

PHOTOGRAPHERS

◆ OVERVIEW

Photographers take and sometimes develop and print pictures of people, places, objects, and events. They use a variety of cameras and photographic equipment to record events, capture a mood, or tell a story. Photographers usually specialize in one of several areas: portraiture, commercial and advertising photography, photojournalism, fine art photography, educational photography, or scientific photography.

Photographers may work for a newspaper or magazine, advertising or stock photo agency, corporation, association, or government agency. In addition, they may write for trade and technical journals, teach in schools and colleges, sell photographic equipment and supplies, produce documentary films, or do freelance work.

EARNINGS

In the late 1990s, a photographer who handled a routine amount of work earned an average of about $24,800 a year. Photographers who did difficult or challenging work averaged approximately $37,200 a year. Beginning photographers working for newspapers earned an annual median salary of about $19,000; experienced newspaper photographers, a median of $30,700 a year; and the top 10 percent of experienced newspaper photographers, in excess of $38,900 annually. Photographers in government service earned an average salary of about $29,500 a year.

Scientific photographers usually start at salaries higher than other photographers. Self-employed photographers often earn more than salaried photographers, but their earnings depend on general business conditions.

OUTLOOK

Employment of photographers will increase more slowly than the average for all occupations through the year 2008, according to the *Occupational Outlook Handbook*. The demand for new images should remain strong in education, communication, entertainment, marketing, and research. As more newspapers and magazines turn to electronic publishing, the need for photographs should increase.

Digital photography, which involves recording images electronically and downloading them to a computer, is changing the nature of photography in electronic publishing, advertising, and other industries.

Photography is a highly competitive field. There are far more photographers than positions available. Generally only those who are extremely talented and highly skilled can support themselves as self-employed photographers.

 T R A I N I N G

A college education is not required to become a photographer, although college training offers the most promising assurance of success in fields such as industrial, news, or scientific photography. Associate, bachelor's, and master's degrees in photography are all available.

Prospective photographers should have a broad technical understanding of photography plus as much practical experience with cameras as possible. A knowledge of developing, printing, and photo manipulation is also valuable.

Students who hope to become photographers should possess manual dexterity, good eyesight and color vision, and artistic ability. In addition, you should be patient and attentive to detail.

E X P L O R I N G

Photography is a field that almost anyone with a camera can explore. Students can join high school camera clubs, school yearbook or newspaper staffs, and community hobby groups to gain experience. A part-time or summer job at a camera shop or photo-processing laboratory will offer additional insight. Finally, try entering photography contests to see how others rate your work.

R E S O U R C E S

National Press Photographers Association
3200 Croasdaile Drive, Suite 306
Durham, NC 27705
Tel: 800-289-6772
Web: http://metalab.unc.edu/nppa/index.html

Professional Photographers of America
229 Peachtree Street, NE, No. 2200
Atlanta, GA 30303-2206
Tel: 404-522-8600
Web: http://www.ppa-world.org

REPORTERS

OVERVIEW

Reporters gather and analyze information on newsworthy events and write stories for newspaper or magazine publication or for radio or television broadcast. The stories may provide information about local, regional, national, or international events, or they may present points of view on issues of current interest. In this latter capacity, the press plays an important role in monitoring the actions of public officials and others in positions of power. A reporter's goal is to cover a story objectively and impartially.

Stories may originate as an assignment from an editor or as a lead. Reporters interview people, observe events as they happen, and do background research. Then they organize their material into a story, including writing and sometimes helping to edit video footage. Many reporters work in satellite locations and send their stories via computer modem to the paper or station they represent.

EARNINGS

In the late 1990s, reporters on daily newspapers having Newspaper Guild contracts received starting salaries ranging from about $10,000 to $68,000 annually, depending on the size of the city. The average starting salary was about $25,000. Reporters with two to six years of experience earned salaries from $18,000 to $70,000.

The *Occupational Outlook Handbook* cited a 1996 survey by the National Association of Radio Broadcasters, which found average annual salaries for radio reporters to fall between $20,217 and $38,541. Reporters who worked in television earned between $17,000 and $75,000. High-profile columnists and newscasters working for prestigious papers or network television stations earned more than $100,000 a year.

✦ OUTLOOK

The employment outlook for reporters and correspondents through 2008 is expected to grow somewhat slower than the average for all occupations. According to Bureau of Labor Statistics projections, the number of employed reporters and correspondents is projected to decline by about 3 percent within the next several years. While the number of self-employed reporters and correspondents is expected to grow, newspaper jobs are expected to decrease. Smaller newspapers will offer the best opportunities for beginners. The bright spot in this field is the growth in online media, which is expected to offer numerous job opportunities in the near future.

✦ TRAINING

At least a bachelor's degree is essential for aspiring reporters. Most editors prefer applicants with a degree in journalism. Journalism courses and programs are offered by many colleges and universities as well as some community and junior colleges. Graduate degrees give students entering the field a great advantage.

Reporters must be inquisitive, assertive, persistent, and detail-oriented and should enjoy interacting with different types of people. Computer skills are essential. Knowledge of speedwriting or shorthand and a familiarity with photography and printing are helpful.

✦ EXPLORING

To explore this field, start by talking to reporters at local newspapers and radio and television stations—or interviewing the admissions counselor at the school of journalism closest to your home. You can also work on your high school or college newspaper or on the newsletter for a local organization. College students might seek out jobs as campus correspondents for area newspapers. Many newspapers and magazines offer summer internships to journalism students, which provide practical experience as well as good contacts.

✦ RESOURCES

Association for Education in Journalism and Mass Communication
234 Outlet Pointe Boulevard
Columbia, SC 29210-5667
Tel: 803-798-0271
Web: http://www.aejmc.org

Dow Jones Newspaper Fund
PO Box 300
Princeton, NJ 08543-0300
Tel: 609-452-2820
Web: http://www.dj.com/newsfund

National Association of Broadcasters
1771 N Street, NW
Washington, DC 20036
Tel: 202-429-5300
Web: http://www.nab.org

WRITERS

◆ OVERVIEW

Writers work in the field of communications. They deal with the written word, whether it is destined for the printed page, broadcast, computer screen, or live theater. The nature of their work is as varied as the materials they produce: books, magazines, trade journals, newspapers, technical reports, company newsletters and other publications, advertisements, speeches, scripts for motion picture and stage productions, and material for radio and television broadcasts. Writers develop ideas and write for all media. They can be employed either as in-house staff or as freelancers.

EARNINGS

In the late 1990s, beginning writers and researchers received starting salaries of about $21,000 a year, according to the Dow Jones Newspaper Fund. Experienced writers and researchers are paid $30,000 and over, depending on their qualifications and the size of the publication they work on. In general, the median beginning wage for those with a college degree is $28,600 per year. The salaries of experienced writers ranges from about $45,000 to over $67,000 per year. Earnings of those in supervisory positions are on the higher end, as are the salaries of technical writers.

In addition to their salaries, many writers earn income from freelance work. Part-time freelancers may earn from $5,000 to $15,000 a year. Full-time established freelance writers may earn up to $75,000 a year.

OUTLOOK

The employment of writers is expected to increase faster than the average rate of all occupations through 2008. The demand for writers by newspapers, periodicals, book publishers, and nonprofit organizations is expected to increase. Advertising and public relations will also provide job opportunities.

Competition for jobs in this field is extremely keen. Opportunities tend to be best in firms that prepare business and trade publications and in technical writing.

◆ TRAINING

Writing jobs almost always demand a college education. Employers often prefer those with degrees in communications or journalism, but a broad liberal arts background can make you equally marketable. Occasionally a master's degree in a specialized writing field may be required. Writers who specialize in technical fields may need degrees, concentrated course work, or experience in specific subject areas such as engineering, business, or one of the sciences.

Writers should be creative and able to express ideas clearly, have a broad general knowledge, be skilled in research techniques, and be computer literate. Other assets include curiosity, persistence, initiative, and the ability to thrive in a deadline-oriented environment.

 ## EXPLORING

As a high school or college student, you can test your interest and aptitude in this field by reporting or writing for school newspapers, yearbooks, and literary magazines. Small community newspapers and local radio stations often welcome contributions from outside sources, although they may not have the resources to pay for them. Jobs in bookstores offer a chance to become familiar with various publications. Information on careers in writing may also be obtained by visiting local newspapers, publishers, or radio or television stations and interviewing writers who work there. Career conferences frequently include speakers on the entire field of communications.

 ## RESOURCES

National Association of Science Writers
PO Box 294
Greenlawn, NY 11740
Tel: 516-757-5664

National Conference of Editorial Writers
6223 Executive Boulevard
Rockville, MD 20852
Tel: 301-984-3015
Web: http://www.ncew.org

National Writers Union
Web: http://www.nwu.org

The Writers' Union of Canada
National Office
24 Ryerson Avenue
Toronto, ON, M5T 2P3, Canada
Tel: 416-703-8982
Web: http://www.swifty.com/twuc/

66*Extracurricular activities are essential
to being a well-rounded student.* 99
*– Andrea D. Bashara,
Assistant Dean for Admissions and Student Services,
Creighton University School of Law, Omaha, Nebraska*

66*We view extracurricular activities in concert
with the academic record, but the academic profile
always takes precedence. If, however, we are considering
a group of students with similar strong academic qualifications,
the ones with the more highly rated extracurricular accomplishments
will have a stronger chance of admission.* 99
*– Connie Sheehy,
Associate Director of Admission,
Williams College, Williamstown, Massachusetts*

Science Clubs

✦ INTRODUCTION

Are you the kind of person who likes to figure out how things work? Are you interested in why it rains, or how a fossil from the ocean floor ends up on a mountain thousands of miles from water? Maybe you find it fascinating to examine materials through a microscope. If so, you might have the makings of a scientist.

The careers in this chapter deal with science and its many dimensions. From the study of rocks and minerals to the origins of human life, science seeks answers to the questions people have been asking for thousands of years—and many new ones, such as in the field of genetics.

As you read through these entries, consider your natural curiosities and talents. Perhaps you'll end up experimenting with a career in science.

AGRICULTURAL SCIENTISTS

◇ OVERVIEW

Agricultural scientists study all aspects of living organisms and the relationships of plants and animals to their environment. They conduct research and
apply the results to such tasks as increasing crop yields and improving the environment. Some agricultural scientists plan and administer programs for testing
foods, drugs, and other products. Others direct activities for public exhibits at
zoos and botanical gardens, teach at colleges and universities, work as consultants
to businesses and the government, or design and develop agricultural equipment
aimed at boosting production. Much of the research conducted by agricultural
scientists is done in laboratories, but some is carried out in the field. A botanist
may have occasion to examine the plants that grow in the volcanic valleys of
Alaska, while an animal breeder might study the behavior of animals on the
plains of Africa.

◇ EARNINGS

A 1998 *R&D Magazine* survey found that technicians working in the field of
biology earn about $46,027 a year; researchers with a doctorate earned $59,079
annually. Salaries in engineering varied from $36,610 for technicians to $54,160
for researchers and $84,020 for research and development directors. Agricultural
scientists working for the government can enter the field making between $26,000
and $35,000 a year. Those in government jobs with doctorates and more experi-
ence might make between $67,000 and $87,000.

✦ OUTLOOK

A recent decrease in enrollment in schools of agricultural science will mean
more job opportunities for those who graduate. Those with doctorates will have
the most opportunities, but those with bachelor's and master's degrees will also
find work as technicians or in farm management.

The fields of biotechnology and genetics may hold the best opportunities
for agricultural scientists. New developments, such as methods of processing corn
for use in medicines, will alter the marketplace. Scientists will also be increasingly
involved in improving the environmental impact of farming as well as crop yields.

◆ TRAINING

To become an agricultural scientist, you should pursue a college degree related to agricultural and biological science. A doctorate is usually mandatory for college or university professors, independent researchers, and field managers. A bachelor's degree may be acceptable for some entry-level jobs, such as testing or inspecting technicians, but advancement opportunities are limited without an advanced degree.

Some attributes necessary for jobs in this field are the ability to work effectively alone as well as part of a team, a curiosity about the nature of living things and their environment, a strong concentration level, and physical stamina (for those scientists who do field research in remote areas of the world).

◆ EXPLORING

If you live in an agricultural community, you have a good chance of finding part-time or summer work on a farm or ranch. A Future Farmers of America or 4-H program will introduce you to the concerns of farmers and researchers and may involve you directly in science projects. Contact your county's extension office to learn about regional projects. Also helpful would be part-time or volunteer work at a veterinarian's office, florist, landscape nursery, orchard, zoo, animal shelter, aquarium, botanical garden, or museum.

◆ RESOURCES

American Dairy Science Association
1111 North Dunlap Avenue
Savoy, IL 61874
Tel: 217-356-3182
Web: http://www.adsa.uiuc.edu

American Society of Agricultural Engineering
2950 Niles Road
St. Joseph, MI 49085
Tel: 616-429-0300
Web: http://asae.org

American Society of Agronomy
677 South Segoe Road
Madison, WI 53711
Tel: 608-273-8095
Web: http://www.agronomy.org

ASTRONOMERS

OVERVIEW

Astronomers study the universe and its celestial bodies by collecting and ana-lyzing data. They make statistical studies of stars and galaxies and prepare math-ematical tables giving positions of the sun, moon, planets, and stars at a given time. They also study the size and shape of the earth and the properties of its upper atmosphere through observation and data collected by spacecraft and earth satellites.

Astronomers typically specialize in a particular branch of their field. For example, the astrophysicist is concerned with applying the concepts of physics to stellar atmospheres and interiors. Radio astronomers study the source and nature of celestial radio waves with highly sensitive radio telescopes.

The majority of astronomers either teach or do research or a combination of both. Other astronomers are engaged in such activities as the development of astronomical instruments, administration, technical writing, and consulting.

EARNINGS

According to a 1998 survey by the Commission on Professionals in Science and Technology, professionals holding doctoral degrees in earth and space sci-ences averaged $33,000 for nine-month contracts in educational institutions. Salaries for space professionals in business and industry were higher, with an average salary of $58,600. The average for space professionals employed by the government was $47,500.

The American Institute of Physics reported a median salary of $70,000 in 1998 for its members with PhDs; $57,000 for master's degree professionals; and $54,000 for those with bachelor's degrees. Government pay for astronomy and space scientists was $81,300 a year in 1999.

Private industry consulting fees run as high as $200 per day in specialized fields of astronomy.

✦ OUTLOOK

Astronomy is one of the smallest science fields, and competition for astron-omy-related jobs will continue to be strong. In recent years, the number of new openings in this field have not kept pace with the number of astronomers gradu-ating from the universities, and this trend is likely to continue for the near future.

The federal government will continue to provide employment opportunities for astronomers. However, government agencies, particularly NASA, may find their budgets reduced in the coming years, and the number of new positions created for astronomers will likely drop as well.

The greatest growth in employment of astronomers is expected to occur in business and industry. Companies in the aerospace field will need astronomers to help them develop new equipment and technology.

◆ TRAINING

All astronomers are required to have some postsecondary training, with a doctoral degree being the usual educational requirement. A master's degree is sufficient for some jobs in applied research and development, and a bachelor's degree is adequate for some nonresearch jobs. Students should select a college program with wide offerings in physics, mathematics, and astronomy and should take as many of these courses as possible. Graduate training will normally take about three years beyond the bachelor's degree. Some graduate schools require that an applicant for a doctorate spend several months in residence at an observatory.

The field of astronomy calls for people with a strong but controlled imagination, the ability to see relationships between what may appear to be unrelated facts and form hypotheses about these relationships, and the ability to concentrate for long periods of time.

◆ EXPLORING

A number of summer or part-time jobs are usually available in observatories, some as guides or assistants to astronomers. These jobs not only offer experience in astronomy but often act as stepping stones to good jobs upon graduation. Students also can test their interest in this field by working part-time or volunteering at a planetarium or science museum.

Many people enjoy astronomy as a hobby, and there are a number of amateur astronomy clubs and groups active throughout the country. Purchasing or even building your own telescope will give you experience in studying the skies.

◆ RESOURCES

Amateur Astronomers Association
1010 Park Avenue
New York, NY 10028
Tel: 212-535-2922
Web: http://www.aaa.org

American Astronomical Society

2000 Florida Avenue, Suite 400
Washington, DC 20009
Tel: 202-328-2010
Web: http://www.aas.org

American Institute of Physics

1 Physics Ellipse
College Park, MD 20740-3843
Tel: 301-209-3100
Web: http://www.aip.org

Astronomical Society of the Pacific

390 Ashton Avenue
San Francisco, CA 94112
Tel: 415-337-1100
Web: http://www.aspsky.org

NASA Web Site

http://www.nasa.gov/

BIOLOGISTS AND MARINE BIOLOGISTS

OVERVIEW

Biologists study the origin, development, anatomy, function, distribution, and other basic principles of living organisms, including humans, microorganisms, plants, and animals. They are concerned with the nature of life itself and with the relationship of each organism to its environment. Biologists perform research in many specialties that advance the fields of medicine, agriculture, and industry. These include botany (the study of plants), microbiology (the study of microorganisms), zoology (the study of animals), and many more. Nearly a quarter of all biologists work in government jobs.

Marine biologists study species of plants and animals living in oceans, their interactions with one another, and how they influence and are influenced by environmental factors. They generally work either in a laboratory setting or in the field, which in this case means on or near the ocean.

EARNINGS

Salaries for all biological scientists range from $22,000 to over $66,000, with a median salary of $36,300, according to the US Department of Labor. In 1997, biologists with bachelor's degrees who worked for the federal government earned average salaries of $52,100 a year. According to the National Association of Colleges and Employers, average beginning salaries in 1997 ranged from $25,400 to $52,400 a year.

Based on information from the American Society of Limnology and Oceanography, marine biologists with bachelor's degrees and no experience might find a federal government job that pays between $21,000 and $33,000. Those with doctoral degrees in marine biology can earn as much as $80,000. Senior scientists and full professors at universities can make more than $100,000.

✦ OUTLOOK

A faster-than-average increase in employment of biologists is predicted for the next few years, although competition will be stiff for high-paying jobs, and government jobs will be less plentiful—and less secure since they are often contingent on funding. Advances in genetic research and expanded medical research should open up some opportunities, and private industry will need more biologists to keep up with the advances in biotechnology. Efforts to preserve and clean up the environment will create more job opportunities for qualified biologists.

Many colleges and universities are cutting back on their faculties, but high schools and two-year colleges may have teaching positions available.

There are more marine biologists than there are paying positions at present. Changes in the earth's environment will most likely prompt more research and result in slightly more jobs in different subfields. The need for better management of the world's fisheries, research by pharmaceutical companies into deriving medicines from marine organisms, and cultivation of marine food alternatives are other factors that may increase the demand for marine biologists in the near future.

✦ TRAINING

The best way to prepare for a career as a biologist is to earn a bachelor's degree in biology or one of its specialized fields, such as anatomy or botany. For the highest professional status, a doctorate is required. This is particularly true for top research positions and most higher-level college teaching openings.

A state license may be required for biologists who are employed as technicians in general service health organizations, such as hospitals or clinics. You also must be licensed if you'll be handling hazardous materials in a lab.

Although it is possible to get a job as a marine biologist with just a bachelor's degree, most marine biologists have a master's or doctoral degree.

If you are going to be diving, organizations like the Professional Association of Diving Instructors provide basic certification. Training for scientific diving is more in-depth and requires passing an exam and fulfilling other criteria.

Biologists must be analytical and systematic in their approach to solving problems, have an inquisitive but patient nature, and be able to communicate well. The job of marine biologist—which often involves scuba diving and hiking on uneven terrain, for example—requires strength and physical endurance.

✦ EXPLORING

School assemblies, field trips to laboratories and research centers, and professional conferences can provide insight into the field of biology. Part-time and summer positions in biology or related areas are also helpful. Students with some college courses in biology may find positions as laboratory assistants. Graduate students may find work on research projects conducted by their institutions. High school students often have the opportunity to join volunteer service groups at local hospitals. Student science training programs allow qualified high school students to spend a summer doing research under the supervision of a scientist.

A volunteer or paid position at a local aquarium is an excellent way to learn about marine life and the field of marine biology. You can plan ahead by beginning diving training while in high school.

✦ RESOURCES

American Institute of Biological Sciences
1444 I Street, NW, Suite 200
Washington, DC 20005
Tel: 202-628-1500
Web: http://www.aibs.org

American Society for Microbiology
Office of Education and Training—Career Information
1325 Massachusetts Avenue, NW
Washington, DC 20005-4171
Tel: 202-737-3600
Web: http://www.asmusa.org

American Society of Limnology and Oceanography
5400 Bosque Boulevard, Suite 680
Waco, Texas 76710-4446
Tel: 800-929-2756
Web: http://www.aslo.org

Biotechnology Industry Organization
1625 K Street, NW, Suite 1100
Washington, DC 20006
Tel: 202-857-0244
Web: http://www.bio.org

CHEMISTS AND BIOCHEMISTS

◆ OVERVIEW

Chemists are scientists who study the composition, changes, reactions, and transformations of matter. They may specialize in analytical, biological, inorganic, organic, or physical chemistry. More than half of all chemists work in research and development laboratories. Research in chemistry falls into two categories: basic and applied. Basic research entails searching for new knowledge about chemicals and chemical properties. In applied research, chemists use the knowledge obtained from basic research to create new and/or better products for use by consumers or in manufacturing processes, such as the development of new pharmaceuticals for the treatment of a disease or superior plastics for space travel. Other jobs in the chemistry field include teaching, marketing, sales, and manufacturing quality control and production.

Biological chemists, also known as *biochemists,* examine the chemical compositions and reactions in living organisms. They identify and analyze the chemical processes involved in such functions as growth, metabolism, reproduction, and heredity. They also study the effect of environment on living tissue. Biochemists are generally employed in one of three areas: medicine, nutrition, or agriculture.

◆ EARNINGS

In 1998, the lowest third of salaries for all chemists was about $31,000 a year. A midrange salary for the field was $60,000, and a high salary was about $97,000 a year. According to a membership survey by the American Chemical Society in 1998, the median salary for all industrial chemists was $69,500; for those with government jobs, $64,100; and for those in academia, $54,000.

Salaries in 1998 for biochemists working for the federal government ranged from about $21,000 to about $101,000. A report from the American Chemical Society cited a salary range of $47,251 to $79,176 for biochemists working in industry jobs.

◆ OUTLOOK

The outlook for the field of chemistry is expected to be particularly good for researchers interested in working in pharmaceutical firms, biotechnology firms, and firms producing specialty chemicals. However, growth is expected to decrease in the industrial chemical and oil industries. Overall, the total number of chemists employed is forecast to increase by about 14 percent from 1998 to

2008. A well-trained chemist should have little trouble finding some type of employment in the field.

The prospects for biochemists through 2008 are also good, and career prospects are bright for those training in any of the molecular life sciences. Although funding cuts threaten the field's long-term growth prospects, ample employment opportunities should continue to be available in health research and genetic engineering, at least in the near future. College and university jobs for doctoral degree holders should also be plentiful.

✦ TRAINING

The minimum educational requirement for a chemist or biochemist is a bachelor's degree in science. However, in the upper levels of basic and applied research, and especially in a university setting, most positions are filled by people with doctoral degrees.

Upon entering college, students majoring in chemistry should expect to take classes in several branches of the field, such as organic, inorganic, analytical, physical, and biochemistry. Chemistry majors also must advance their skills in mathematics, physics, and biology and be proficient with computers.

If you wish to go into biochemistry but your institution does not offer a specific program in biochemistry, you may (1) work toward a bachelor's degree in chemistry and take courses in biology, molecular genetics, and biochemistry, including a biochemistry laboratory class, or (2) earn a bachelor's degree in biology but take more chemistry, mathematics, and physics courses than the biology major requires and choose a biochemistry course that involves lab work. Graduate schools prefer students with laboratory or research experience.

Chemists must be detail-oriented, precise, patient workers. They should also be inquisitive, work effectively alone or in groups, be self-motivated, and communicate well.

✦ EXPLORING

Chemistry and biology classes offer the best means of exploring a career in chemistry or biochemistry while still in high school. These courses offer students the opportunity to learn scientific methods, perform chemical and biological experiments, and become familiar with terminology. Contact the department of chemistry or biology at a local college or university to discuss the field with an instructor and arrange a tour of their laboratory or classroom. Manufacturers and research institutions may employ students in their laboratories, but it can be difficult for high school students to get a summer job or internship because of the extensive training involved. Some community colleges train students as laboratory technicians.

✦ **RESOURCES**

American Association for Clinical Chemistry
2101 L Street, NW, Suite 202
Washington, DC 20037-1526
Tel: 202-857-0717 or 800-892-1400
Web: http://www.aacc.org

American Chemical Society
Department of Career Services
1155 16th Street, NW
Washington, DC 20036
Tel: 202-872-4600
Web: http://www.acs.org

American Society for Biochemistry and Molecular Biology
Education Information
9650 Rockville Pike
Bethesda, MD 20814-3996
Tel: 301-530-7145

FORESTERS AND FORESTRY TECHNICIANS

✦ OVERVIEW

Foresters protect, develop, and manage forests—one of our greatest natural resources. Using their specialized knowledge of tree biology and ecology, wood science, and manufacturing processes, they manage forests for timber production, protect them from fire and pest damage, direct the harvesting of mature forests, and supervise the planting and growing of new trees after harvesting. They also manage forests for recreational and educational purposes, working to minimize the environmental impact.

Forestry technicians work as members of a forest management team under the direction of a forester. They survey land, collect data and information, create charts and maps, mark trees for cutting, control fires, operate logging equipment, and handle other tasks involved in maintaining and protecting forests.

✦ EARNINGS

According to the *Occupational Outlook Handbook,* foresters employed by the federal government earned average starting salaries ranging from $19,500 to $42,900 in 1997, depending on their education level. The average federal salary for a forester in 1997 was $47,600. Experienced foresters can make up to $75,000. Starting salaries in private industry are comparable to starting salaries in the federal government.

✦ OUTLOOK

According to the US Bureau of Labor Statistics, employment of foresters is expected to increase about as fast as the average for all occupations through the year 2008. Budgetary limitations have led to cutbacks in federal programs, where employment is concentrated. Prospects for foresters outside the federal government are expected to be better, however. Demand at the state and local level should continue to increase, due to emphasis on environmental protection and responsible land management. Some growth is also expected in private industry, which may need additional personnel to improve logging and milling practices in order to reduce waste.

A promising area for prospective forestry technicians is forest recreation, including hunting and fishing. Growing numbers of people are enjoying the forests, and their resources must be well managed and protected.

TRAINING

The minimal educational requirement for a career as a forester is a bachelor's degree in forestry; however, some foresters combine three years of liberal arts education with two years of professional education in forestry and receive the degrees of bachelor of arts and master of forestry. Those who wish to specialize in a certain area or broaden their general knowledge of forestry may opt for graduate work toward a master's degree or doctorate.

Prospective forestry technicians usually take a two-year program that leads to an associate degree, either at a technical institute or a junior or community college. In some states, forestry technicians need to be licensed to perform certain duties.

To pursue a career in forestry, you should have a scientific mind, an enthusiasm for outdoor work, good physical health and stamina, and the ability to work effectively in emergency situations. You should also be self-sufficient, resourceful, and able to work well without supervision.

EXPLORING

One way to explore the field of forestry is to talk with someone working as a forester or forestry technician. In some parts of the country, local chapters of the Society of American Foresters invite prospective forestry students to some of their meetings and field trips.

If you live near a forested area, you might be able to find a summer or part-time forestry job. Unskilled workers are sometimes needed, and this type of hands-on work would be a good introduction to the field.

◆ RESOURCES

American Forests
PO Box 2000
Washington, DC 20013
Tel: 202-955-4500
Web: http://www.amfor.org

Canadian Forestry Association
185 Somerset Street West, Suite 203
Ottawa, ON, K2P OJ2, Canada
Tel: 613-232-1815

Society of American Foresters
5400 Grosvenor Lane
Bethesda, MD 20814-2198
Tel: 301-897-8720
Web: http://www.safnet.org

GENETIC SCIENTISTS

✦ OVERVIEW

Genetic scientists, or *geneticists,* study heredity. They study plants as well as animals, including humans. Genetic scientists conduct research on how characteristics are passed from one generation to the next through the genes present in each cell of an organism. This research often involves manipulating or altering particular genetic characteristics to better understand how genetic systems work. For instance, a genetic scientist may breed a family of mice with a tendency toward high blood pressure to test the effects of exercise or diet on that condition. The ultimate goal of genetic scientists is to increase biological knowledge so as to understand and cure genetic diseases, predict birth defects and genetic disorders in unborn babies, and breed new crops and livestock, among other things.

Genetics is a component of just about every area of biology and can be found in many biology subfields. Rapidly growing specialty areas include genetic counseling and medical genetics.

✦ EARNINGS

Starting salaries in 1998 for genetic scientists who went to work for the federal government ranged from $21,421 to $39,270, depending on their education level. In 1995, the average salary for genetic scientists working in private industry was around $51,404, with biotechnology firms offering higher salaries. The highest paid, most experienced genetic scientists made upwards of $70,000 to $80,000 a year. Universities, which generally hire only geneticists with doctoral degrees, paid salaries ranging from $31,000 for new assistant professors to $51,500 for full professors.

✦ OUTLOOK

Interest in the field of genetic research has exploded in the past five years, with breakthrough discoveries bringing greater attention to the possibilities for finding genetic causes and cures for diseases. In fact, it is estimated that every human disease that is caused by a single gene defect will be curable by genetic intervention during the lifetime of students currently in high school.

A survey conducted by the American Association for the Advancement of Science asked its 2,500 members to name the scientific specialty with the most promise for the next decade. Genetics was listed as the number one choice by biologists, physicists and astronomers, social and behavioral scientists, and chemists. It was listed as the second most promising field by medical scientists, engineers, and earth scientists.

With the demand for genetic scientists expected to significantly increase, this field will grow much faster than the average.

 ## TRAINING

A college degree is necessary for a career as a genetic scientist. A major in biology or genetics, supplemented by courses in math, chemistry, and physics, is recommended. Those with bachelor's or master's degrees should find ample job opportunities in the rapidly growing biotechnology field. Research technicians are needed in that industry, as well as in government jobs. A doctoral degree is needed if you aim to teach at a college or university or work as a clinical geneticist.

Geneticists must be inquisitive and have the ability to think scientifically. Their long hours of laboratory work demand patience and persistence. This work also requires strong communication skills as well as the ability to be sensitive and diplomatic.

 ## EXPLORING

High school science teachers can often contact departments of biology and genetics at nearby colleges and universities and arrange field trips or speakers. They can also get information about university summer programs. If you wish to explore a career in genetics, take advantage of these and other opportunities offered through community colleges, museums, professional associations, and special interest groups.

RESOURCES

American Society of Human Genetics
9650 Rockville Pike
Bethesda, MD 20814-3998
Tel: 301-571-1825
Web: http://www.faseb.org/genetics

Genetics Society of America
9650 Rockville Pike
Bethesda, MD 20814
Tel: 301-571-1825
Web: http://www.faseb.org/genetics

National Society of Genetic Counselors
233 Canterbury Drive
Wallingford, PA 19086
Tel: 610-872-7608

GEOLOGISTS AND GEOLOGICAL TECHNICIANS

✦ OVERVIEW

Geologists study all aspects of the earth, including its origin, history, composition, and structure. This includes the exploration of a wide variety of phenomena, such as mountain and rock formations, mineral deposition, earthquakes, and volcanic eruptions. Geologists also use theoretical knowledge and research data to locate groundwater, oil, minerals, and other natural resources. They play an increasingly important role in studying, preserving, and cleaning up the environment. They advise construction companies and government agencies on the suitability of locations being considered for buildings, highways, and other structures. They also prepare geological reports, maps, and diagrams for a variety of purposes.

Geological technicians assist geologists in their studies and field work, either working under the supervision of a geologist or as part of a research team. Their duties include drafting maps, analyzing and interpreting raw data, and writing reports.

Geologists and geological technicians may spend several months per year doing field work. They also work in laboratories.

✦ EARNINGS

Beginning geologists earn about $30,900 a year on the average; those with master's and doctoral degrees earn more. Salaries vary widely depending on the employing industry. For example, the average starting salary in the oil and gas industry is approximately $48,400 for those with bachelor's degrees, while geologists with bachelor's degrees employed in research or teaching typically start out making less. In the federal government, average salaries for geologists range from about $54,800 to about $67,000.

According to an industry survey, entry-level geological technicians in the private sector can expect to earn an average of $20,000 a year, while those with extensive experience earn an average of $45,000. The average salary for a geological technician working for the federal government in 1997 was $45,000.

✦ OUTLOOK

In response to curtailed petroleum activity in the late 1980s and 1990s, the number of graduates in geology and geophysics, especially petroleum geology, has dropped considerably in the last decade. Stability has now returned to the petroleum industry, increasing the need for qualified geoscientists. With new technologies and greater demand for energy resources, job opportunities are expected to be good, especially for those with master's degrees and those familiar with computer modeling and GPS (global positioning system).

According to the *Occupational Outlook Handbook,* employment of geologists and geological technicians is expected to grow about as fast as the average for all occupations through the year 2008. In addition to the oil and gas industries, jobs will be available in environmental protection and reclamation. Government agencies will have fewer job openings because of funding cutbacks.

TRAINING

A bachelor's degree is the minimum requirement for entry into lower-level geology jobs, but a master's degree is usually necessary for beginning positions in research, teaching, or exploration. For those wishing to make significant advancements in research and college-level teaching, a doctoral degree is needed.

A high school diploma is recommended for anyone considering a career as a geological technician. Though not required, postsecondary education is helpful; some companies will not hire technicians without a degree. A bachelor of science degree with an emphasis in geology, advanced mathematics, and drafting is recommended. Some two-year colleges offer an associate degree for geological technicians.

Those interested in the geological profession should have an aptitude not only for geology but also for physics, chemistry, and mathematics. Computer modeling, data processing, and effective communication skills are important, and physical stamina is needed for those involved in field work. Geological technicians must be highly detail-oriented and able to interpret data accurately.

EXPLORING

Students interested in a career in geology should read as much as possible about geology and geologists. It would also be helpful to take a college course in geology, such as mineralogy or physical geology. Science teachers and museums are other good sources of information. Large oil and gas companies, such as Chevron, Texaco, and Shell, may be able to provide insight into careers in the geological sciences, and some of these companies offer educational programs for high school students and opportunities for summer employment. Joining a geology or rock collecting club or organization will also give you good exposure to the field.

◆ RESOURCES

American Geological Institute

4220 King Street
Alexandria, VA 22302
Tel: 703-379-2480
Web: http://www.agiweb.org

American Institute of Professional Geologists

7828 Vance Drive, Suite 103
Arvada, CO 80003-2125
Tel: 303-431-0831
Web: http://www.aipg.org

Association of Engineering Geologists

Department of Geology and Geophysics
Texas A&M University, MS-3115
College Station, TX 77843-3115
Tel: 409-845-0142
Web: http://aegweb.org

Geological Society of America

3300 Penrose Place
Boulder, CO 80301-9140
Tel: 303-447-2020
Web: http://www.geosociety.org

METEOROLOGISTS

 OVERVIEW

Meteorologists study the earth's atmosphere to forecast weather conditions and changes. By analyzing weather maps and related charts, as well as interpreting reports from observers, weather satellites, weather radar, and remote sensors, they can predict the movement of fronts, precipitation, and pressure areas. They also forecast temperature, wind velocity, and humidity levels.

To predict future weather patterns and to develop increased accuracy in weather study and forecasting, meteorologists conduct research on subjects ranging from radioactive fallout to the dynamics of hurricanes to ocean currents. The work of meteorologists also contributes to air-pollution control, transportation and defense strategies, agricultural production, and environmental preservation efforts.

The National Weather Service employs the most meteorologists, followed by the Department of Defense and the armed forces. Other meteorologists work for radio and television stations, weather consulting firms, and airlines as well as in teaching jobs.

 EARNINGS

The salaries of meteorologists depend on the amount of training they have and the setting in which they are employed. The average salary of meteorologists employed by the federal government is about $50,500 a year. Starting salaries for government meteorologists with a bachelor's degree range from $19,500 to $24,200; with a master's degree, $24,200 to $29,600; and with a doctoral degree, $35,800 to $42,900.

In broadcast meteorology, salaries vary greatly. Starting salaries begin at $20,000 a year, experienced meteorologists average $46,000 per year, and in large media markets some broadcast meteorologists earn over $100,000 annually.

✦ OUTLOOK

According to the *Occupational Outlook Handbook,* employment for meteorologists is expected to grow more slowly than the average for all other occupations through the next decade. Competition for jobs is stiff, and employment of meteorologists by federal agencies is expected to decline as the federal government balances its budget.

✦ TRAINING

Although some beginners in meteorological work have majored in subjects related to meteorology, the normal minimal requirement for work in this field is a bachelor's degree in meteorology from one of the almost 100 colleges offering a major in this field. The federal government, for example, requires beginners to have had a minimum of 20 semester hours in meteorology, supplemented by work in physics and differential and integral calculus. Advanced graduate training in meteorology and related areas is required for research and teaching positions, as well as for other high-level positions in meteorology. Doctorates are common among high-level personnel.

Meteorologists must be able to work well under pressure and clearly communicate complex theories and results, both verbally and in writing.

✦ EXPLORING

Students who are interested in meteorology can explore the field in several ways. Each year the National Weather Service accepts a limited number of student volunteers, mostly college students but also a few high school students. Some universities offer credit for a student's volunteer work in connection with meteorology courses. The National Oceanographic and Atmospheric Administration has details about the volunteer program. The armed forces can also be a means of gaining experience in meteorology. Or try interviewing a meteorologist to learn about the career firsthand.

✦ RESOURCES

American Meteorological Society
45 Beacon Street
Boston, MA 02108
Tel: 617-227-2425
Web: http://www.ametsoc.org

National Oceanographic and Atmospheric Administration
US Department of Commerce
14th Street and Constitution Avenue, Room 6013
Washington, DC 20230
Tel: 202-482-6090
Web: http://www.noaa.gov

National Weather Association
6704 Wolke Court
Montgomery, AL 36116-2134
Tel: 334-213-0388

OCEANOGRAPHERS

OVERVIEW

Oceanographers obtain information about the ocean through observations, surveys, and experiments. They study the physical, chemical, and biological composition of the ocean and the geological structure of seabeds, including the motions of ocean water (waves, currents, and tides), marine life (sea plants and animals and their habits), ore and petroleum deposits (minerals and oils contained in the nodules and oozes of the ocean floor), and the contour of the ocean floor (ocean mountains, valleys, and depths). Many of their findings are compiled for maps, charts, graphs, and special reports and manuals.

Oceanographers typically spend some of their time on the water each year gathering data and making observations. Additional oceanographic work is done on land. Experiments using models or captive organisms are often conducted in seaside laboratories.

Oceanographers are usually part of a highly skilled team, with each member specializing in a different aspect of the field.

EARNINGS

According to a 1996 report by the National Association of Colleges and Employers, those graduating with a bachelor's degree in geology and geological sciences were offered an average starting salary of $32,091. In 1995, the average annual salary for experienced oceanographers was $58,980.

In 1998, oceanographers working for the federal government earned starting salaries ranging from $21,421 to $47,066, depending on their education level.

In addition to their regular salaries, oceanographers may supplement their incomes with fees from consulting, lecturing, and publishing their findings.

◆ OUTLOOK

Although the field of marine science is growing, researchers specializing in the popular field of biological oceanography, or marine biology, will face competition for available positions and research funding over the next few years. However, funding for graduate students and professional positions is expected to increase during the coming decade in the areas of global climate change, environmental research and management, fisheries science, and marine biomedical and pharmaceutical research programs.

In general, oceanographers who also have training in other sciences or in engineering will probably have better opportunities for employment than those with training limited to oceanography. Those with less education will have opportunities for employment as assistants or technicians; job opportunities are currently good, though increasingly competitive, for marine technicians.

 TRAINING

A college degree is required even for beginning positions in oceanography. A broad program covering the basic sciences with a major in physics, chemistry, biology, or geology is desirable. In addition, you should take courses that involve field research or laboratory work in oceanography where available. Graduate work in oceanography is required for most positions in research and teaching.

Personal traits helpful for a career in oceanography are a strong interest in science (including observing nature and performing experiments), outdoor activities, and academics, as well as an eye for detail and above-average verbal, numerical, and spatial aptitudes.

 EXPLORING

Opportunities for exploring the field of oceanography include work in marine or conservation fisheries or on board seagoing vessels, or field experience studying rocks, minerals, or aquatic life. Volunteer work for students is often available with research teams, nonprofit organizations, and public facilities such as aquariums. If you live in a coastal region, you will have an easier time becoming familiar with oceans and ocean life than if you are land-bound. However, you can still gain exposure by learning all you can about the geology, atmosphere, and plant and animal life of the area where you live, regardless of whether water is present. Another idea is to find a summer internship, camp, or program that involves travel to a coastal area.

RESOURCES
About Oceanography
Texas Sea Grant College Program
Texas A&M University
PO Box 1675
Galveston, TX 77553-1675
Web: http://www-ocean.tamu.edu/Careers/careers.html
Ocean Engineering Society
Institute of Electrical and Electronics Engineers
345 East 47th Street
New York, NY 10017-2394

Scripps Institution of Oceanography
0-233 University of California, San Diego
9500 Gilman Drive
La Jolla, CA 92093-0233
Web: http://www.sio.ucsd.edu

The Oceanography Society
4052 Timber Ridge Drive
Virginia Beach, VA 23455
Tel: 757-464-0131
Web: http://www.tos.org/

PALEONTOLOGISTS

 OVERVIEW

Paleontologists study the fossils of ancient life-forms, including human life, found in sedimentary rocks on or within the earth's crust. Paleontological analyses range from the description of large, easily visible features to biochemical analysis of incompletely fossilized tissue. The observations are used to infer relationships between past and present groups of organisms, to investigate the origins of life, and to explore the ecology of the past, from which implications for the sustainability of life under present ecological conditions can be drawn. Paleontology is usually considered a subspecialty of the larger field of geology—essentially it is geology's biological branch.

Paleontologists can be found working in universities, with consulting companies, as museum curators, in federal and provincial surveys, and in the petroleum and mining industries—their findings are helpful in identifying oil reservoirs and mineral deposits.

◆ **EARNINGS**

The American Geological Institute estimates that an experienced professional with a bachelor's degree in the geological sciences can make about $40,000 a year; those with doctorates can average as high as $77,000 a year. According to a 1998 salary survey by the American Association of University Professors, salaries for professors ranged from $45,163 to $61,816, depending on the level of the institution. A 1997 survey by the American Association of Petroleum Geologists found that those professionals in the petroleum industry with only a few years' experience averaged $51,300 a year, while those with 10 to 20 years of experience averaged between $78,000 and $90,000 annually.

◆ **OUTLOOK**

More paleontologists graduate each year than there are available positions, and consequently many paleontologists are unemployed or underemployed. As the energy sector moves overseas, fewer jobs are available in the domestic fossil fuels industry. Federal and state surveys absorb a small number of new graduates with bachelor's or master's degrees but cannot accommodate all those seeking work. Educational opportunities are also diminishing as colleges and universities eliminate and scale back their science departments.

To increase the likelihood of employment, students should pursue independent research and publication during the advanced degree years; cross-train in a related field, such as zoology or botany; and plan a broad-based career that includes government and industry activities as well as teaching and research.

◆ TRAINING

For a career in paleontology, you will want to major in geology or biology in college, supplemented by courses in math, science, history, and computers. While it is not strictly necessary, most scientists in the paleontology field find that a doctorate is necessary simply to have time to gain the substantial knowledge base and independent research skills required to be successful.

An inquisitive nature, a strong interest in science and history, a respect for other cultures, strong organizational skills, and the ability to work well with others are traits typical of a paleontologist.

◆ EXPLORING

An estimated 55,000 amateur "rock hounds" belong to organized clubs in the US that are devoted to hunting for fossils. You could locate and join one of these clubs or take fossil-hunting expeditions on your own. Professional geology societies publish brochures on fossil hunting and the kinds of fossils available in different locales. Visiting museums is also helpful; some museums with a strong geology component conduct field trips that are open to the public.

State geological societies, often housed on the main campuses of state universities, are excellent sources of information, as is Earthwatch, an organization that involves people with environmental projects.

◆ RESOURCES

American Geological Institute
4220 King Street
Alexandria, VA 22302
Tel: 703-379-2480
Web: http://www.agiweb.org

Paleontological Research Institution
1259 Trumansburg Road
Ithaca, NY 14850
Tel: 607-273-6623
Web: http://www.englib.cornell.edu/pri

PHARMACOLOGISTS

OVERVIEW

Pharmacologists play an important role in medicine and in science by studying the effects of drugs, chemicals, and other substances on humans and animals. These highly educated specialists perform laboratory research to determine how drugs and other materials act at the cellular level and how they affect living organs and tissues and vital life processes. They design the chemical agents that cure, lessen, or prevent disease, including studying potentially harmful side effects and recommending proper dosages.

Pharmacologists are increasingly involved in toxicological research, studying materials used in the environment, agriculture, and industry. They identify toxic substances in workplaces, pesticides, food preservatives, and such household items as paints, aerosol sprays, and cleaning fluids.

Pharmacology is often confused with pharmacy, but the two are not the same. Pharmacy is the health profession responsible for the preparation and dispensing of drugs to patients.

EARNINGS

According to the *Hospital Salary and Benefits Report* published in 1997, directors of pharmacy (positions frequently held by pharmacologists) have annual salaries ranging from $43,680 to $111,379, with a national average of $69,316. A survey by the American Association of Pharmaceutical Scientists placed average salaries at $70,000 a year for those working in industry, $66,400 for those in academia, and $62,500 for those in government. Higher-salaried pharmacologists are typically those who supervise teams of people in laboratory or university settings or who serve as senior faculty in academic departments.

✦ OUTLOOK

Health care and health care-related industries are expected to continue to expand, which means that the activities of drug companies; hospitals; medical, dental, and pharmacy schools; and the government in pharmacological research will continue to be strong. The growing elderly population will also mean more drug production and development. A number of medical conditions and diseases will require the continuing and increasing expertise of pharmacologists, including the development of drugs to fight AIDS, muscular dystrophy, and cancer, as well as those to facilitate organ transplants. The expanding field of gene therapy and the growing area of herbal pharmacology are expected to offer additional opportunities. More teachers of pharmacology will also be needed.

◆ TRAINING

Nearly all pharmacologists earn a PhD, and some also have doctoral degrees in medicine or veterinary medicine. The PhD in pharmacology is usually earned at an accredited medical school or accredited school of pharmacy. The PhD program requires four to five years of study, often followed by two to four years of additional research training.

Pharmacologists are creative, innovative thinkers who communicate well and are patient and persistent enough to invest long hours—often working alone—on research that does not provide quick or easy answers.

◆ EXPLORING

The best way for you to learn about pharmacology is to interview pharmacologists. Your high school counselor or science teacher may be able to arrange a talk by a qualified pharmacologist or even a tour of a pharmacological facility.

Medical and other laboratories frequently employ part-time personnel, and it is sometimes possible to secure a part-time job in a pharmacological laboratory. Information regarding summer or part-time opportunities can be obtained by contacting work-study or student research programs and student placement services.

◆ RESOURCES

American Association of Pharmaceutical Scientists
2107 Wilson Boulevard, Suite 700
Arlington, VA 22201-3046
Tel: 703-243-2800
Web: http://www.aaps.org

American Society for Pharmacology and Experimental Therapeutics
9650 Rockville Pike
Bethesda, MD 20814-3995
Tel: 301-530-7060
Web: http://www.faseb.org/aspet

ROBOTICS ENGINEERS AND TECHNICIANS

OVERVIEW

Robotics engineers design, develop, build, and program robots and robotic devices, including peripheral equipment and computer software used to control robots. Robotics engineers have a thorough understanding of robotic systems and equipment and available technologies, as well as a strong foundation in computer systems and how computers are linked to robots. They evaluate manufacturing operating systems and production requirements to determine how robots can best be used in automated systems to achieve cost efficiency, productivity, and quality.

Robotics technicians assist robotics engineers in a wide variety of tasks relating to the design, development, production, testing, operation, repair, and maintenance of robots and robotic devices.

EARNINGS

Earnings and benefits in manufacturing companies vary widely, but in general, engineers with a bachelor of science degree earn annual salaries between $32,000 and $35,000 in their first job after graduation. Engineers with several years of experience earn salaries ranging from $35,000 to $60,000 a year.

Robotics technicians who are graduates of a two-year technical program earn between $22,000 and $26,000 a year, and those with special skills or more experience can earn $36,000 or more. Technicians involved in design and training generally earn the highest salaries, with experienced workers earning $45,000 or more a year.

✦ OUTLOOK

After a slump of several years, it is predicted that the robotics industry will once again pick up. The use of industrial robots is expected to grow as robots become more programmable and flexible and as manufacturing processes become more automated. Growth is also expected in nontraditional applications, such as education, health care, security, and nonindustrial purposes.

It is difficult to predict whether recent sales and the rising production of robots will increase employment opportunities, but trends for automated manufacturing equipment and a willingness by manufacturers to invest in capital expenditures are promising signs. For prospective robotics engineers and technicians, this suggests that more workers will be needed to design, build, install, maintain, and operate robots.

TRAINING

Because changes occur so rapidly within this field, it is often recommended that engineers and technicians get a broad-based education, in automated manufacturing, for example, which includes robotics, electronics, and computer science.

In order to become an engineer, it is necessary to earn a bachelor of science degree. For some higher-level jobs, such as robotics designer, a master of science or doctoral degree is required.

Although the minimum educational requirement for a robotics technician is a high school diploma, many employers prefer to hire technicians who have received formal training beyond high school. Two-year associate degree programs are available at community colleges and technical institutes, and technical programs are available through the armed forces.

Good manual dexterity, hand-eye coordination, and mechanical and electrical aptitudes are some of the skills needed in this field.

EXPLORING

Because robotics is such a new field, if you are interested in this career, it is important to learn as much as possible about current trends and recent technologies. You can do this by reading books and trade magazines and attending trade shows.

You can also become a robot hobbyist and build your own robot or buy toy robots and experiment with them. There are even competitions for students, like one sponsored by the Robotics International of the Society of Manufacturing Engineers for middle school through university-level students.

Other suggested activities include membership in your high school science club, participation in science fairs, and hobbies that involve electronics, mechanical equipment, and model building.

◆ RESOURCES

Association for Unmanned Vehicle Systems
1735 North Lynn Street, Suite 950
Arlington, VA 22209
Tel: 703-524-6646

Robotics and Automation Council

Institute of Electrical and Electronics Engineers
Education Information
345 East 47th Street
New York, NY 10017
Tel: 212-705-7900
Web: http://www.ieee.org

Robotic Industries Association

900 Victors Way
PO Box 3724
Ann Arbor, MI 48106
Tel: 734-994-6088
Web: http://www.robotics.org

Society of Manufacturing Engineers

Education Department
PO Box 930
Dearborn, MI 48121-0930
Tel: 800-733-4763
Web: http://www.sme.org

SOIL CONSERVATIONISTS AND TECHNICIANS

OVERVIEW

Soil conservationists develop conservation plans to help landowners and operators—such as farmers and ranchers, developers, homeowners, and government officials—best use and manage their land while maintaining sound conservation practices and adhering to government regulations. Assessing the land users' needs and costs, they suggest plans to conserve and reclaim soil (including the rotation of crops, which also increases yields), preserve or restore wetlands and other ecosystems, reduce water pollution, and restore or increase wildlife populations. They obtain data and design project specifications using survey and field information, technical guides, and engineering field manuals.

Soil conservation technicians work more directly with land users by putting the ideas and plans of conservationists into action. They perform engineering surveys and design and implement conservation practices like terraces and grassed waterways. Soil conservation technicians monitor projects during construction and periodically revisit sites for evaluation.

EARNINGS

The majority of soil conservationists and technicians work for the federal government, and their salaries are determined by their government service rating. In 1997, the average annual salary for soil conservationists employed by the federal government was $45,200, according to the *Occupational Outlook Handbook*. Those with bachelor's degrees started at $19,500 or $24,200 a year depending on academic achievement; a master's degree, $24,200 or $29,600; and a doctorate, $35,800. The salaries of workers employed by state and local governments vary widely.

Soil conservation technicians, who do not usually have college degrees, earn starting salaries of $15,500 per year.

The annual salaries of conservationists and technicians working for private firms or agencies range from about $19,000 to about $70,000.

◆ OUTLOOK

Most soil conservationists and technicians are employed by the federal government; therefore, employment opportunities will depend largely on levels of government spending. It is always difficult to predict future government policies; however, this is an area where the need for government involvement is apparent and pressing. The vast majority of America's cropland has suffered from some sort of erosion, and only continued efforts by soil conservation professionals can prevent a dangerous depletion of our most valuable resource—fertile soil.

Decreased levels of employment by the federal government could lead to increased employment opportunities at public utility companies, banks and loan agencies, state and local governments, and mining and steel companies.

Overall, it is anticipated that this field will grow about as fast as the average.

✦ TRAINING

The federal government requires soil conservationists to earn at least 30 college credit hours and have significant work experience in order to be considered for a position. A bachelor's degree in agronomy, agricultural education, range management, forestry, or agricultural engineering is especially helpful to the aspiring soil conservationist. Some conservationists may consider earning a master's degree in a natural resources field.

A college education is not required of soil conservation technicians.

A love for the outdoors, a scientific mind, and the ability to clearly convey technical information are attributes necessary for jobs in this field.

✦ EXPLORING

One of the best ways for you to become acquainted with soil conservation work and technology is through summer or part-time work on a farm. Other ways to explore this career include joining a 4-H Club or the Future Farmers of America. Science courses that include lab sections, and mathematics courses that focus on practical problem-solving will also give you a feel for this kind of work.

✦ RESOURCES

American Society of Agronomy
Career Development and Placement Service
677 South Segoe Road
Madison, WI 53711
Tel: 608-273-8080
Web: http://www.agronomy.org

Natural Resources Conservation Service
US Department of Agriculture
Attn: Conservation Communications Staff
PO Box 2890
Washington, DC 20013
Web: http://www.nrcs.usda.gov/

Soil and Water Conservation Society
7515 NE Ankeny Road
Ankeny, IA 50021
Tel: 515-289-2331
Web: http://www.swcs.org/

SOIL SCIENTISTS

✦ OVERVIEW

Soil scientists study the physical, chemical, biological, and mineralogical characteristics and behaviors of soils. They determine the origin, distribution, composition, and classification of soils so that they may be put to the most productive and effective use. Soil scientists do some of their work outdoors, surveying fields, assessing drainage, studying plant life, and collecting soil samples. And all soil scientists work in the laboratory. They make chemical analyses of the soil and examine samples under the microscope to determine their components. With their findings, they can advise farmers and other landowners on crop production, soil fertility, and soil management. A number of soil scientists with advanced degrees teach and conduct research projects in colleges of agriculture.

✦ EARNINGS

According to the US Department of Labor, the average pay for soil scientists in 1997 was $49,400 a year. Soil scientists working for the government can enter the field making between $26,000 and $35,000 a year. Those with doctorates and a great deal of experience may make between $67,000 and $87,000.

✦ OUTLOOK

According to the *Occupational Outlook Handbook,* employment of agricultural scientists, which includes soil scientists, is expected to grow about as fast as the average for all occupations through the year 2008. The Handbook reports that agricultural scientists will be needed to balance increased agricultural output with protection and preservation of soil, water, and ecosystems.

Technological advances, such as computer programs and new methods of conservation, will allow scientists to better protect the environment while also improving farm production. One of the challenges facing future soil scientists will be convincing farmers to change their current methods of tilling and chemical treatment in favor of environmentally safer methods.

✦ TRAINING

A bachelor's degree in agronomy or soil science is the minimum educational requirement to become a soil scientist. To direct and administer research programs or to teach at the university level, soil scientists usually need doctoral degrees. Master's degrees are helpful for many research positions.

It's good to have some farm experience or background before going into soil science. You should also be able to work effectively alone and with others, have good communication and computer skills, and be tolerant of long hours of work outdoors.

✦ EXPLORING

If you live in an agricultural community, you should be able to find part-time or summer work on a farm or ranch. A Future Farmers of America program will introduce you to the concerns of farmers and researchers. A local 4-H club can also give you valuable experience in the agricultural arena. Contact your county's soil conservation department or related government agency to learn about regional projects.

✦ RESOURCES

National Society of Consulting Soil Scientists
325 Pennsylvania Avenue, SE, Suite 700
Washington, DC 20003
Tel: 800-535-7148
Web: http://www.nscss.org

Soil Science Society of America
677 South Segoe Road
Madison, WI 53711
Tel: 608-273-8095
Web: http://www.soils.org

CHAPTER 9

Speech and Debate

"Generally, students who have been involved in extracurricular activities tend to have better class participation and peer involvement."

– Cora Mae Haskell, Registrar/Dean of Student Services,
Si Tanka College, Eagle Butte, South Dakota

✦ INTRODUCTION

Do you like to discuss your feelings and ideas with classmates, friends, your family? Do you enjoy the challenge of persuading people to see things from your point of view? Maybe you have a gift for teaching or instructing others. Why not put these skills of discourse to use in your career?

From religious ministries to lawyers, the jobs in this chapter are as diverse as the points of view in a debate or political campaign. Whether it's in the business world, the educational arena, or a community church, our society needs charismatic, eloquent people to lead us, inform us, and persuade us.

Maybe one of these careers will speak to you.

CLERGY

✦ OVERVIEW

Clergy are religious leaders who provide for the spiritual, educational, and social needs of congregations and other people of the community. They lead services, interpret doctrine, perform religious rites, and provide moral and spiritual guidance to their members. Clergy also help the sick and needy, supervise educational programs, and sometimes have administrative duties. They may also be involved in missionary work.

This article will focus on three of the many types of clergy: Protestant ministers, rabbis, and Roman Catholic priests.

✦ EARNINGS

Salaries for Protestant clergy vary depending on the person's experience and the church's denomination, size, location, and financial status. The estimated average income of ministers is about $27,000 per year. Additional benefits usually include a housing stipend, a monthly transportation allowance, and health insurance, which can raise the average compensation for senior pastors in large congregations to over $50,000. Other benefits may bring that number even higher. Some ministers of smaller congregations add to their earnings by working at part-time secular jobs.

Salaries for rabbis vary according to the size, branch, location, and financial status of their congregations. Information is limited, but the earnings of rabbis tend to range from $30,000 to $80,000. Smaller congregations offer salaries on the lower end of the scale, usually between $30,000 and $50,000 a year. Some congregations may allow their rabbi to teach at local universities or other settings to earn additional income.

Roman Catholic priests take a vow of poverty and are supported by their orders. Any salary that they receive for writing or other activities is usually turned over to their religious orders. Diocesan priests (those leading small parishes within a certain diocese) receive small salaries calculated to cover their basic needs. These salaries average about $9,000 a year but vary according to the size of the parish, its location, and its financial status. Additional benefits usually include a monthly travel allowance, room and board in the parish rectory, car allowance, health insurance, retirement benefits, and educational allowance. Priests who teach or do specialized work usually receive a small stipend that is less than that paid to lay persons in similar positions. Priests who serve in the armed forces receive the same amount of pay as other officers of equal rank.

✦ OUTLOOK

While overall membership in Protestant churches is growing, most of the mainline denominations, such as the Baptist, Lutheran, Methodist, and Presbyterian churches, are not. Aging membership and a significant increase in nondenominational congregations has caused church budgets and membership to shrink, lessening the demand for full-time ministers. Overall, the increased cost of church operations is expected to limit the demand for Protestant ministers. Graduates of theological schools have the best prospects for employment, as do ministers willing to work in rural churches with smaller congregations, salaries, and benefits.

Job opportunities for rabbis are generally good, but the availability of positions varies with the branch of Judaism to which a rabbi belongs. Orthodox rabbis should have fairly good job prospects as older rabbis retire and smaller communities become large enough to hire their own rabbi. Conservative and Reform rabbis should also have good employment opportunities, especially because of retirement and new Jewish communities. Reconstructionist rabbis should find very good opportunities because this branch of Judaism is growing rapidly. Small communities offer the best opportunities.

Opportunities for positions in the priesthood are increasing and will probably continue to do so for the foreseeable future. There is a shortage of priests; in the last 30 years, the number of priests has declined by about 25 percent because of retirement and those leaving the profession for other reasons. Priests are needed in all areas of the country, but the greatest need is in metropolitan areas that have large Catholic populations and in communities near Catholic educational institutions.

✦ TRAINING

While some denominations require little more than a high school education or Bible study, the majority of Protestant groups require a bachelor's degree—typically in the liberal arts—plus several years of specialized theological training. Theological study generally lasts about three years and leads to the degree of Master of Divinity. The major Protestant denominations have their own schools of theological training, but many of these schools admit students of other denominations. There are also several interdenominational colleges and theological schools that give training for the ministry. Protestant ministers must meet the requirements of their individual denominations.

Completion of a course of study in a seminary is a prerequisite for ordination as a rabbi. Entrance requirements, curriculum, and length of seminary program vary depending on the particular branch of Judaism. Prospective rabbis normally need to complete a bachelor's degree before entering the seminary. Degrees in Jewish studies, philosophy, English, or history can fulfill seminary entrance requirements. It is advisable to study Hebrew at the undergraduate level. Most seminary programs lead to the Master of Arts in Hebrew Letters degree and ordination as a rabbi. Most programs last about five years, and many of them include a period of study in Jerusalem.

Eight years of post-high-school study are usually required to become an ordained priest. Candidates for the priesthood often choose to enter at the college level or begin their studies in theological seminaries after college graduation. The additional four years of preparation for ordination are given over entirely to the study of theology, including field work in community parishes. Postgraduate work in theology and other fields is available and encouraged for priests, who may study in American Catholic universities, ecclesiastical universities in Rome, or other places around the world.

The personal requirements for clergy are typically the same, regardless of denomination. They need a strong religious faith and desire to help others; other interests and potential vocations should be considered secondary to their calling. They should be outgoing and friendly and able to get along with people from a wide variety of backgrounds. They need patience, compassion, and open-mindedness to interact with those who seek their counsel, as well as the ability to be respectful and discreet. Leadership qualities are also important, including self-confidence, initiative, strong presentation skills, and the ability to supervise others.

◆ EXPLORING

The first step in exploring this career is to speak with your own minister, rabbi, or priest. He or she can tell you more about it, help you discern your own calling, and put you in touch with other people and resources. It also makes sense to become as involved with your congregation as possible: teaching Sunday school, attending weekly services and religious study groups, and helping with special events or administrative work. You might also want to volunteer to visit with the sick or the elderly, particularly in institutions affiliated with your church or synagogue. You can also visit a seminary to get a better idea of what the vocation is all about.

If you are specifically interested in becoming a Catholic priest, you might wish to spend time in a monastery; many monasteries are open to the public for weekend or even weeklong retreats.

◆ RESOURCES

Evangelical Lutheran Church in America
8765 West Higgins Road
Chicago, IL 60631
Tel: 800-638-3522
Web: http://www.elca.org

Jewish Theological Seminary of America
3080 Broadway
New York, NY 10027
Tel: 212-678-8000
Web: http://www.jtsa.edu/

National Religious Vocation Conference (Catholic)
5420 South Cornell Avenue, Suite 105
Chicago, IL 60615
Tel: 773-363-5454
Web: http://www.visionguide.org

Presbyterian Church (USA)
100 Witherspoon Street
Louisville, KY 40202
Tel: 800-872-3283
Web: http://www.pcusa.org/

Southern Baptist Convention
901 Commerce
Nashville, TN 37203
Tel: 615-244-2355
Web: http://www.sbc.net

United Methodist Church
Board of Higher Education and Ministry
PO Box 871
Nashville, TN 37202
Tel: 615-340-7356
Web: http://www.umc.org or http://www.gbhem.org/

COLLEGE AND UNIVERSITY PROFESSORS

◇ OVERVIEW

College and *university professors* instruct undergraduate and graduate students in specific subjects at colleges and universities. They are responsible for conducting classes, including lecturing, leading seminars and discussions, assigning reading and research projects, and administering exams. Though many professors spend fewer than 10 hours a week in the classroom, they spend many hours preparing lectures and lesson plans and grading papers and exams. They also schedule office hours during the week to be available to students outside the classroom. Many also serve as student advisers.

College and university faculty also study and consult with colleagues to keep up with the latest information in their fields. They conduct ongoing research and often publish their theories and findings in journals and textbooks.

◇ EARNINGS

Both the *Chronicle of Higher Education* and the American Association of University Professors (AAUP) conduct annual surveys of the salaries of college professors. With the 1998 survey, the *Chronicle* found that full professors at public universities received an average of $69,924 a year, while professors at private universities received $84,970 a year. Associate professors received an average of $50,186 annually at public universities and $56,517 at private. For assistant professors, the average salaries were $42,335 at public universities and $47,387 at private.

The AAUP survey found that professors in doctoral institutions made an average of $61,816 a year, compared to $50,243 for those in master's institutions and $45,163 for those in undergraduate institutions.

✦ OUTLOOK

According to the *Occupational Outlook Handbook,* employment of college and university faculty is expected to increase faster than the average for all occupations through 2008, as enrollments in higher education increase. Many openings will arise as current faculty retire. But pressured to cut costs, many colleges and universities are replacing tenure-track faculty positions with part-time instructorships that can be filled by adjunct faculty, visiting professors, and graduate students.

The best teaching opportunities are expected to be in the fields of business, computer science, engineering, and health science—those that offer attractive nonacademic job opportunities, thereby creating less competition for academic positions.

 TRAINING

At least one advanced degree in your field of study is required to be a professor in a college or university. The master's degree is considered the minimum standard, and graduate work beyond the master's is usually desirable. A doctorate is typically required to advance beyond instructor (to assistant professor, associate professor, or professor), especially at four-year institutions.

You should enjoy reading, writing, and researching, because your whole career will be based on communicating your thoughts and ideas. People skills are important because you'll be dealing directly with students, administrators, and other faculty members on a daily basis. You should feel comfortable in a role of authority and possess self-confidence.

 EXPLORING

Your high school teachers use many of the same skills as college professors, so talk to your teachers about their careers and their college experiences. You can gain teaching experience by working at a community center, day care center, or summer camp. Spend some time on a college campus to get a sense of the environment. Write to colleges for their admissions brochures and course catalogs; read about the faculty members and the courses they teach. Before visiting college campuses, make arrangements to speak to professors who teach courses that interest you. These professors may allow you to sit in on their classes and observe.

 RESOURCES

American Association of University Professors
1012 14th Street, NW, Suite 500
Washington, DC 20005
Tel: 202-737-5900
Web: http://www.aaup.org

American Federation of Teachers
555 New Jersey Avenue, NW
Washington, DC 20001
Tel: 202-879-4400
Web: http://www.aft.org

LAWYERS AND JUDGES

✦ OVERVIEW

Lawyers, also called *attorneys,* serve as advocates and advisors in our legal system. As advocates, they represent the rights of their clients in trials and depositions or in front of administrative and government bodies. As advisors, attorneys counsel clients on how the law affects business or personal decisions, such as the purchase of property or the creation of a will. Lawyers represent individuals, businesses, and corporations.

Judges are elected or appointed officials who preside over federal, state, county, and municipal courts. They apply the law to citizens and businesses and oversee court proceedings according to established law. Judges also make new rulings on issues not previously decided.

EARNINGS

In 1996, according to the National Association for Law Placement, the starting salary for federal government lawyers was approximately $34,500. Average starting salaries for lawyers in business was nearly $45,000. The 1996 average for lawyers in private industry was about $60,000 annually, although some senior partners earned well over $1 million a year. General attorneys in the federal government received an average of about $72,000. Patent attorneys in the federal government averaged around $81,600.

According to the Administrative Office of the US Courts, in 1996 federal district court judges averaged $133,600 and federal circuit court judges, $141,700. The chief justice of the United States earned $171,500, while associate justices of the Supreme Court earned $164,100. A survey conducted by the National Center for State Courts reported that the 1997 salary average for state intermediate appellate court judges was $91,000; state associate justices earned $101,800.

OUTLOOK

The demand for lawyers is expected to grow as fast as the average through the year 2008. The US Department of Labor predicts that 119,000 new positions will be added between the years 1998 and 2008—a 16-percent increase in employment. However, record numbers of law school graduates have created strong competition for jobs, even though the number of graduates has begun to level off. The best opportunities exist in small towns or suburbs of large cities, where there is less competition.

Employment of judges is expected to grow more slowly through the year 2008, according to the US Department of Labor. Judges who retire, however, will need to be replaced. There may be an increase in judges in cities with large population growth, but competition will be high for any openings.

 TRAINING

To enter any law school approved by the American Bar Association, you must satisfactorily complete at least three and usually four years of college work. Most law schools do not specify any particular prerequisites, but a liberal arts track is most advisable. Law students considering specialization, research, or teaching may go on for advanced study.

Every state requires that lawyers be admitted to the bar of that state before they can practice. They require that applicants graduate from an approved law school and that they pass a written examination in the state in which they intend to practice.

Nearly all judges appointed or elected to any court must be lawyers and members of the bar, usually with many years of experience.

 EXPLORING

If you think a career as a lawyer or judge might be for you, sit in on a trial or two at your local or state courthouse. Talk to your guidance counselor about setting up an informational interview with a judge or lawyer. A shadowing program would allow you to follow a lawyer or judge around for a day or two to get an idea of what goes on in a typical day. You may even be invited to help out with a few minor duties.

 RESOURCES

American Bar Association
Information Services
750 North Lake Shore Drive
Chicago, IL 60611
Tel: 312-988-5000
Web: http://www.abanet.org

Federal Bar Association
Student Services
2215 M Street, NW
Washington, DC 20037
Tel: 202-785-1614
Web: http://fedbar.org

US Court of Appeals for the Federal Circuit

717 Madison Place, NW
Washington, DC 20439
Tel: 202-633-6550
Web: http://www.fedcir.gov

PRESS SECRETARIES AND POLITICAL CONSULTANTS

◆ OVERVIEW

Press secretaries and *political consultants* help politicians promote themselves and their issues among voters, using the media to either change or strengthen public opinion. They advise politicians on how to address the media and they develop media campaigns—a series of television ads, for example—to help politicians get elected. These professionals are often called spin doctors because of their ability to manipulate the media or put a good spin on a news story to best suit the purposes of their clients.

Press secretaries work for candidates and elected officials, while political consultants work with firms, contracting their services to politicians. The majority of press secretaries and political consultants work in Washington, DC; others work throughout the country for local and state government officials and candidates.

◆ EARNINGS

Press secretaries working in the US Congress can make between $42,000 and $60,000 a year, according to the Congressional Management Foundation, a consulting firm in Washington, DC. The incomes of political consultants vary greatly: Someone contracting with local candidates or state organizations and associations may make around $40,000 a year, while a consultant for a high-profile candidate may bring in hundreds of thousands of dollars a year. In a 1998 Pew Research Center study, more than half of the respondents reported family incomes of more than $150,000 a year; a third reported annual incomes of more than $200,000.

◆ OUTLOOK

This field is expected to grow about as fast as the average. As more news networks and news magazines closely follow the decisions and actions of elected officials, press secretaries and political consultants will become increasingly important. The Pew Research Center, which surveys the public on political issues, has found that most Americans are concerned about negative campaigning, but it remains a very effective tool for consultants. In some local elections, candidates may mutually agree to avoid mud-slinging, but the use of negative ads in general is likely to increase.

Voters will soon be able to access more information about candidates and issues via the Internet. The greater number of outlets for media products, including cable television, will employ more writers, television producers, and Web designers in the process of creating a political campaign.

TRAINING

For a career in this field, you will need a good understanding of the history and culture of the United States as well as other countries. A bachelor's degree is a virtual requirement; many press secretaries and political consultants also hold master's degrees, doctorates, and law degrees. Majors to consider include journalism, political science, English, marketing, and economics. You might pursue graduate study in journalism, political science, public administration, or international relations. A political or journalism internship would also serve you well.

You'll need to be very organized and able to work well under pressure. You'll also need good problem-solving skills, self-confidence, and the ability to handle people well. You should feel comfortable with public speaking and enjoy working in a sometimes competitive arena.

EXPLORING

Get involved with your school government as well as with committees and clubs that have officers and elections. Working for your school newspaper will help you learn about conducting research, interviews, and surveys—all part of managing media relations. You may be able to get a part-time job or an internship with your city's newspaper or radio or television station, where you can gain exposure to election coverage and political advertising. You can also become involved in local, state, and federal elections by volunteering for campaigns.

Visit the Web sites of US Congress members; many sites feature lists of recent press releases. By reading these releases, you'll get a sense of how a press office publicizes the efforts and actions of Congress members.

✦ RESOURCES

Office of Senator (Name)
United States Senate
Washington, DC 20510
Tel: 202-224-3121
Web: http://www.senate.gov

The Pew Research Center for the People and the Press
1150 18th Street, NW, Suite 975
Washington, DC 20036
Tel: 202-293-3126
Web: http://www.people-press.org

US House of Representatives (Name)
Washington, DC 20515
Tel: 202-224-3121
Web: http://www.house.gov

PUBLIC RELATIONS SPECIALISTS

◇ O V E R V I E W

Public relations specialists develop and maintain programs that present a favorable public image for an individual or organization. They provide information to a target audience about a client, its goals and accomplishments, and future plans, developments, or projects. The duties of a public relations (PR) specialist might include writing press releases; pitching stories to the media; arranging for radio and television interviews and press conferences; writing speeches, reports, and other management communications; handling special events; making public appearances; and planning PR strategies.

PR specialists are employed by corporations, government agencies, nonprofit organizations, public relations consulting firms, and advertising agencies. Many work as independent consultants.

◇ E A R N I N G S

A beginning public relations salary might be about $18,000 a year, but within a few years it can increase to $22,000 or more, according to the Public Relations Society of America. Public relations specialists have median annual earnings of about $50,000. Top salaries can approach $150,000.

According to a 1997 salary survey conducted by the International Association of Business Communicators, the annual salaries of account executives in the United States averaged $38,549; PR specialists, $39,287; and independent PR professionals, $46,124. Public affairs specialists in the federal government averaged about $56,700 in 1999.

✦ O U T L O O K

Employment of public relations professionals is expected to grow faster than average for all occupations through the year 2008, according to the US Department of Labor Statistics. Most large companies are expected to expand their public relations activities and create many new opportunities. More and more smaller companies are hiring public relations specialists, adding to the demand for these workers. The hottest industry appears to be high technology, followed closely by health care. Competition will be keen for entry-level PR jobs.

TRAINING

Most people employed in public relations have a college degree. Recommended fields of study include public relations, English, communications, and journalism. A knowledge of business administration is helpful. A graduate degree may be required for managerial positions.

A public relations specialist must be a strong writer and speaker with good interpersonal, leadership, and organizational skills.

 EXPLORING

An internship or part-time job at a PR firm would be a great way to explore this field. Work on a newspaper or at a radio or television station would give insight into communications media. Assisting with a political campaign or working as a page for the US Congress or a state legislature can help students grasp the fundamentals of political and government processes. Retail jobs offer students exposure to the principles of product presentation.

♦ RESOURCES

Canadian Public Relations Society, Inc.
#720, 220 Laurier Avenue West
Ottawa, ON, K1P 5Z9, Canada
Tel: 613-232-1222
Web: http://www.cprs.ca

International Association of Business Communicators
One Halladie Plaza, Suite 600
San Francisco, CA 94102
Tel: 800-776-4222
Web: http://www.iabc.com

Public Relations Society of America
Career Information
33 Irving Place
New York, NY 10003
Tel: 212-995-2230
Web: http://www.prsa.org

RADIO AND TELEVISION ANNOUNCERS

✦ OVERVIEW

Radio and *television announcers* present news, commercials, and other messages from a script. They identify the station, announce station breaks, and introduce and close shows. Interviewing guests, making public service announcements, and conducting panel discussions may also be part of an announcer's job. Smaller stations may have an announcer who performs the functions of reporting, writing, presenting, and commenting on the news as well as introducing network and news service reports.

Newscasters specialize in reporting news, including the facts and sometimes editorial commentary.

✦ EARNINGS

According to a 1998 salary survey by the Radio-Television News Directors Association, there is a wide range of salaries for announcers. For radio reporters and announcers, the median salary was $20,000 with a low of $10,000 and a high of $75,000. For television reporters and announcers, the median salary was $23,000 with a low of $8,000 and a high of $85,000. For both radio and television, salaries are higher in the larger markets. Evening, night, weekend, and holiday duty may provide additional compensation.

✦ OUTLOOK

The US Department of Labor predicts that opportunities for experienced broadcasting personnel will decrease through the year 2008 due to the lack of growth in new radio and television stations. Openings will result mainly from those who leave the industry or the labor force. Competition for these jobs is expected to be stiff. Newscasters who specialize in such areas as business, consumer, and health issues should have an advantage over other job applicants.

✦ TRAINING

Although there are no formal educational requirements for entering the field of radio and television announcing, many stations prefer college-educated applicants. With a broad educational and cultural background, announcers can typically speak on a wider range of topics and improvise better. Interested students should seek out a college or university with a program in broadcast journalism as well as a strong liberal arts core curriculum.

A Federal Communications Commission license or permit is no longer required for broadcasting positions. Union membership may be required for employment with large stations in major cities and is a necessity with the networks.

Announcers need a pleasing voice and personality, good diction and enunciation, and the ability to think quickly on their feet. Aspiring announcers will also need demo video and/or audiotapes to present to prospective employers.

◆ EXPLORING

If a career as an announcer sounds interesting, try to get a summer job at a radio or television station. You may not have the opportunity to broadcast, but you can learn a lot about the field. You can also gain experience working at your college or university radio or television station. Some radio and television stations and cable companies offer internships, scholarships, and fellowships.

◆ RESOURCES

Association of Local Television Stations
1320 19th Street, NW, Suite 300
Washington, DC 20036
Tel: 202-887-1970
Web: http://www.altv.com

National Association of Broadcasters
1771 N Street, NW
Washington, DC 20036-2891
Tel: 202-429-5300
Web: http://www.nab.org

Radio-Television News Directors Association
1000 Connecticut Avenue, NW, Suite 615
Washington, DC 20036-5302
Tel: 202-659-6510
Web: http://www.rtnda.org

SALES REPRESENTATIVES

◆ OVERVIEW

Sales representatives, also called *sales reps,* sell the products and services of companies and organizations. They identify and contact prospective clients, such as retail stores, manufacturers or wholesalers, government agencies, hospitals, and other institutions. They call on these prospective clients and explain or demonstrate the benefits of their products. Once a sale is made, the salesperson often arranges the logistics, including delivery and installation, and follows up to make sure the customer is satisfied. In addition to seeking out new prospects, sales representatives invest time in maintaining relationships with existing customers. Travel is often involved in this job.

EARNINGS

Many beginning sales representatives are paid a salary while receiving their training. After assuming direct responsibility for a sales territory, they may receive only a commission (a fixed percentage of each dollar sold). Also common is a modified commission plan (a lower rate of commission on sales plus a low base salary). Some companies provide bonuses to successful representatives.

Manufacturers' and wholesale sales representatives make between $16,000 and $100,000 a year, with most earning between $23,000 and $47,000 annually. Dartnell Corporation's 1996 Sales Compensation Survey, cited in the *Occupational Outlook Handbook (OOH),* reported that average annual salaries for service sales representatives fell between $36,000 and $63,000. Door-to-door sales workers may make between $12,000 and $20,000 a year.

OUTLOOK

According to the *OOH,* employment of manufacturers' and wholesale sales representatives is expected to grow more slowly than the average for all occupations through the year 2008. Technology has slowed some aspects of the business, now that customers can order goods from suppliers via the Internet, for example. Future opportunities are likely to be best in consumer electronics and computer technology.

The outlook for service sales representatives, on the other hand, is expected to grow much faster than the average as a group. This is due to growth in the services industries, particularly computer and data processing services. But the *OOH* advises that technology also may temper growth in this area—for instance, as laptop computers and other electronic equipment increase sales workers' productivity, fewer workers will be needed.

TRAINING

A high school diploma is the minimum requirement for most sales positions, although an increasing number of salespeople are graduates of two- or four-year colleges. The more complex a product, the greater the likelihood that it will be sold by a college-educated person. Some areas of sales work require specialized college work. Those in engineering sales, for example, usually have a college degree in a relevant engineering field. Studies in English, speech, psychology, marketing, public relations, economics, advertising, finance, accounting, and business law are all helpful for a career in sales.

Sales representatives should be outgoing and enjoy working with people. They must have self-confidence, enthusiasm, and self-discipline.

EXPLORING

If you are interested in a career in sales, you may benefit from part-time or summer work in a retail store. Working as a telemarketer also could be useful.

Some high schools and junior colleges offer programs that combine classroom study with work experience in sales. Students can also take part in sales drives for school or community groups.

Occasionally manufacturers hire college students for summer assignments. A large percentage of students hired for these specialized summer programs become employees after graduation. Some wholesale warehouses also offer temporary or summer positions.

RESOURCES

Direct Marketing Association
Direct Marketing Educational Foundation
1120 Avenue of the Americas
New York, NY 10036
Tel: 212-768-7277
Web: http://www.the-dma.org/

Manufacturers' Agents National Association
PO Box 247
Geneva, IL 60134
Tel: 630-208-1466

National Association of Sales Professionals
Web: http://www.nasp.com

SCHOOL ADMINISTRATORS

◆ OVERVIEW

School administrators are leaders who ensure the smooth, efficient operation of a school or school system. They establish educational standards and goals and develop programs and policies to reach those goals. They also monitor students' progress, train and motivate teachers and other staff, help develop curriculum, prepare budgets, manage student services, and handle parent and community relations. They coordinate and evaluate the activities of their staff to ensure that they meet established objectives.

School administrators include *school district superintendents, assistant superintendents, school principals,* and *assistant principals.* Private schools also have administrators, often known as *school directors* or *headmasters.*

◆ EARNINGS

The Educational Research Service conducted a survey of the salaries of public school administrators for the 1997-98 school year. Assistant principals earned an annual average of $53,206 in elementary schools and $61,000 in high schools. Elementary school principals made about $64,653 a year, while high school principals made $74,380. The average annual salary for a deputy superintendent was $94,400, while superintendents' yearly earnings were $98,100. Superintendents of large school districts can make over $120,000 a year.

◆ OUTLOOK

The employment of school administrators is expected to grow about as fast as the average, according to the *Occupational Outlook Handbook.* While competition for administrative positions in higher education is intense, competition for jobs at the elementary and secondary school level is declining. While more administrators might be needed with school enrollments on the rise, budget constraints are expected to moderate growth in this field.

◆ TRAINING

Principals and assistant principals are generally required to have a master's degree in educational administration, in addition to several years of experience as a classroom teacher. School superintendents typically need graduate training in educational administration, preferably at the doctoral level, as well as previous experience as an administrator.

Licensure of school administrators is mandatory. Requirements to become licensed may include US citizenship or state residency, graduate training in educational administration, experience, and good health and character. In some states, candidates must pass a qualifying examination.

School administrators need strong leadership and communication skills, the ability to get along with different types of people, and a high level of self-confidence.

 EXPLORING

One of the best sources of information on this field is your own teachers and school administrators. Because you'd first work as a teacher before moving into administration, make sure teaching is of interest to you. Talk to your teachers about their work, and offer to assist them with projects before or after school. School counselors can offer vocational guidance, provide occupational materials, and help you plan an appropriate program of study. You can gain direct experience in the education field by working as a counselor at a summer camp or as an aide at a day care center, volunteering to coach a youth athletic team, or tutoring younger students.

 RESOURCES

American Association of School Administrators
1801 North Moore Street
Arlington, VA 22209
Tel: 703-528-0700
Web: http://www.aasa.org

National Association of Elementary School Principals
1615 Duke Street
Alexandria, VA 22314
Tel: 703-684-3345
Web: http://www.naesp.org

National Association of Secondary School Principals
1904 Association Drive
Reston, VA 20191
Tel: 703-860-0200
Web: http://www.nassp.org

"*Students who participate in extracurricular activities tend to have better time-management skills.***"**
— *Jane Goodwin, Director of Admissions,*
Husson College, Bangor, Maine

"*Not all achieve academically.*
Extracurricular activities may give some students the edge
*because it shows a certain level of commitment.***"**
— *Joseph Marrone, Associate Dean of Undergraduate Admissions,*
University of Bridgeport, Bridgeport, Connecticut

CHAPTER 10

Student Government

* I think extracurricular activities are more important than people think, especially at the most selective colleges. Why? Because the vast majority of candidates for admission to these schools are academically acceptable.*

*— Richard Fuller, Dean of Admission and Financial Aid,
Hamilton College, Clinton, New York*

✦ INTRODUCTION

As citizens of a democracy, it is our right—and responsibility—to vote for the officials we think will do the best job governing our cities, our counties, and our country. Elections, especially national ones, are often well publicized and promoted as campaigning candidates do everything they can to garner votes. But what about when politicians are actually in office? The processes of governing and legislating, which affect all of us in our everyday lives, are often not well known or understood.

If these processes interest you, you may be cut out for a career in government. Perhaps you are intrigued by the way elections are run, or maybe you have taken up a social cause in your city. The entries in this chapter show the variety of skills and interests that are needed in government at all levels—city, county, state, and federal.

Maybe one of these careers will get your vote.

CAMPAIGN WORKERS

◆ OVERVIEW

Campaign workers help candidates for government offices get elected. By calling voters, sending out flyers, and advertising through the media, they educate the public about a candidate's strengths and concerns. They also help develop campaign tactics, prepare speeches and press releases, and arrange for public appearances by the candidate. Campaign managers also oversee budgets, expenses, and fund-raising efforts and work with consultants to analyze demographics and public opinion polls. Campaign workers support candidates for mayor, governor, Congress, and president as well as other local, state, and federal offices.

EARNINGS

Campaign workers who answer phones, prepare mailings, and post flyers are generally unpaid. Managers, however, can make around $3,000 a month for their work, or much more when working on a large campaign. A manager overseeing a budget of millions of dollars is paid well, as are consultants. Political consultants can make well over $100,000 a year. These earnings are paid for by the candidate or by donations from campaign supporters.

◆ OUTLOOK

The media is becoming more and more important in political campaigns. Campaign workers in the coming years will need to have an even better understanding of how to use television and radio to garner voter support. Campaign managers will also need to know how to use the Internet effectively. They will be involved in devising new methods of emailing voters and attracting more people to campaign Web sites.

TRAINING

You can volunteer on a campaign, or even manage one, without any college education. Because the level of work consists of making calls and stuffing envelopes, you won't need much training. But to manage a large campaign, or to work as a campaign director for an organization like the Democratic or Republican National Committee, you'll need a four-year college education. Recommended majors include political science, journalism, economics, and history.

Campaign managers should be self-confident, energetic, organized, and analytical. They need to be able to communicate well with others, be assertive, and be able to make quick decisions.

✦ EXPLORING

You can explore this line of work by getting involved with your student government and running for a student council office. You can also volunteer for local political campaigns and advocate for public policy issues of interest to you. You can even participate in national elections by volunteering at your local Democratic or Republican headquarters. Applicable skills can be acquired through an internship or part-time job for a political consulting firm or in the fund-raising department of a nonprofit organization or educational institution.

✦ RESOURCES

Democratic National Committee
430 South Capitol Street, SE
Washington, DC 20003
Tel: 202-863-8000
Web: http://www.democrats.org

Republican National Committee
310 First Street, SE
Washington, DC 20003
Tel: 202-863-8500
Web: http://rnc.org

CITY MANAGERS

◆ OVERVIEW

A *city manager* directs the administration of a city government in accordance with the policies determined by the city council or other elected authority. City managers oversee planning for population growth, crime prevention, street repairs, law enforcement, traffic management, environmental concerns, public health, and other issues. They prepare proposals and budgets and present them to elected officials for their approval. They work closely with urban planners to coordinate new and existing programs. City managers also meet with private and special interest groups to explain programs, policies, and projects.

◆ EARNINGS

According to the results of a survey published in 1997 by the International City/County Management Association, city managers earn an average of $70,541 a year. The average annual salary reported for a county manager was $88,929. Individual earnings, of course, depend on a person's education and experience as well as on the size of the city. In a city with a population of more than one million people, an experienced city manager may earn up to $130,000 a year. In towns with 2,500 residents or fewer, salaries for city managers average $33,000 a year.

◆ OUTLOOK

This field is expected to experience little change or grow more slowly than the average. Although city management is a growing profession, the field is still relatively small. Few job openings are predicted, and applicants with only a bachelor's degree will have difficulty finding employment. Even an entry-level job often requires an advanced degree.

Future city managers will need to focus on imposing clean air regulations, promoting diversity, providing affordable housing, creating new policing methods, and revitalizing old downtown areas.

◆ TRAINING

You'll need at least a bachelor's degree to work as a city manager. Recommended programs include public administration, political science, sociology, and business. A master's degree will make you more marketable.

People planning to enter city management positions frequently must pass civil service examinations. Most positions require knowledge of computerized tax and utility billing, electronic traffic control, and applications of systems analysis to urban problems.

To be a city manager, you should be decisive, confident, diplomatic, and flexible. You must also interact well with people and have strong communication and negotiation skills.

 EXPLORING

You can learn about public administration by becoming involved in student government or by serving as an officer for a school club. A summer job in a local government office can give you a lot of insight into the workings of a city. Work for your school newspaper and you'll learn about budgets, projects, and school administration. An internship with a local newspaper or radio or television station may give you the opportunity to interview the mayor, council members, and/or the city manager about city administration.

 RESOURCES

International City/County Management Association
777 North Capitol Street, NE, Suite 500
Washington, DC 20002-4201
Tel: 202-289-4262
Web: http://www.icma.org

National League of Cities
1301 Pennsylvania Avenue, NW
Washington DC, 20004
Tel: 202-626-3000
Web: http://www.nlc.org

CONGRESSIONAL AIDES

◆ OVERVIEW

Congressional aides staff the offices of the members of the United States Congress. Working for senators and representatives, they assist with a variety of congressional duties, from administrative support to research on legislation. Aides are generally divided into two groupings: personal staff, who deal with matters concerning the home state, and committee staff, whose work is more involved with the construction and passage of legislation. Members of Congress typically have an administrative assistant, legislative assistants, a press secretary, an office manager, a personal secretary, and a legislative correspondent. An aide may work in an office in Washington, DC, or in a local district or state office.

◆ EARNINGS

According to 1996 and 1997 averages compiled by the Congressional Management Foundation, an administrative assistant, or chief of staff, may make up to $110,000 a year working for a senator, and about $85,000 a year working for a representative. The legislative director has the second highest salary, making $83,000 in the Senate, and $52,000 in the House. Personal secretaries for senators make an average of about $47,000. Press secretaries, caseworkers, and office managers average $37,000 to $42,000 a year in the House, while a press secretary for a senator makes about $60,000. Legislative assistants make about $46,000 in the Senate, and $32,000 in the House. Aides who perform clerical duties earn around $23,000.

◆ OUTLOOK

Members of Congress will continue to need aides, but the number of aides hired will be affected by budget constraints and concerns that Congress members rely too much on their staffs. Overall, the outlook for congressional aides is expected to experience little change in the near future. In some offices, aides may be expected to take on more responsibilities. Your experience as an aide will be affected by such things as constituent concerns, the political party in power, and current issues and events. The Internet is dramatically changing the face of this field.

◆ TRAINING

A college degree is needed for a career as a congressional aide; many aides, such as chiefs of staff and legislative directors, have graduate degrees or law degrees. You should look into undergraduate programs in political science, journalism, or economics. Courses in English, foreign languages, government, political theory, international relations, sociology, and public speaking are recommended.

To work as a congressional aide, you'll need strong problem-solving, communication, writing, and leadership skills as well as an even temperament and the ability to work well under pressure. Diplomacy is also important, as you'll be serving a large constituency with widely varying views.

◆ EXPLORING

An extremely valuable—but highly competitive—learning opportunity is working for a summer or a year as a page on Capitol Hill. You can also gain insight into the work of a congressional aide with local efforts, including participating in school government and volunteering to work on a campaign for a local politician. Many local and state governments offer internship opportunities.

◆ RESOURCES

Congressional Management Foundation
513 Capitol Court, NE, Suite 300
Washington, DC 20002
Tel: 202-546-0100
Web: http://www.cmfweb.org

Senate Placement Office
Room SH-142B
Washington, DC 20510
Tel: 202-228-5627

Web Sites of the US House and Senate
http://www.house.gov
http://www.senate.gov

FEDERAL AND STATE OFFICIALS

✦ OVERVIEW

Federal and *state officials* hold positions in the legislative, executive, and judicial branches of government at the state and national levels. They include governors, judges, senators, representatives, and the president and vice president of the country. Government officials act on behalf of their constituents and are responsible for preserving the government against external and domestic threats, supervising and resolving conflicts between public and private interests, regulating the economy, protecting the political and social rights of citizens, and providing goods and services including education and public health. Among other things, officials pass laws, set up social service programs, and allocate taxpayers' money for goods and services.

✦ EARNINGS

In general, salaries for government officials tend to be lower than what they could make in the private sector. According to the National Conference of State Legislatures, state legislators make from $10,000 to $47,000 a year, although in some states they are not paid a salary at all. *The Book of the States* lists salaries of state governors as ranging from $60,000 to $130,000.

According to the Congressional Research Service, senators and representatives receive $136,673 annually. Congressional leaders such as the Speaker of the House and the Senate majority leader receive higher salaries than the other Congress members. The Speaker of the House makes $171,500 a year.

✦ OUTLOOK

This field is expected to experience little change or grow more slowly than the average in the near future. To attract more candidates to run for legislative offices, states may consider salary increases and better benefits for state senators and representatives. But changes in pay and benefits for federal officials are unlikely. An increase in the number of representatives is possible as the US population grows, but would require additional office space and other costly expansions that budgets may not allow.

✦ TRAINING

State and federal legislators come from all walks of life. Some hold master's degrees and doctorates, while others have only a high school education.

Although a majority of government officials hold law degrees, others have undergraduate or graduate degrees in such areas as journalism, economics, political science, history, and English.

Legislators must have a concern for people, the ability to relate well to others and listen to their concerns, a proficiency for debating and expressing opinions, a likable personality, a good temperament, and a strong character.

◆ EXPLORING

The US Congress and some state legislatures offer opportunities for students to work as pages on Capitol Hill for a summer or a year. This position gives firsthand insight into the political process. Many candidates for local and state offices welcome young people to assist with campaigns. State and local officials sometimes offer internships for students. Other ways to learn about government are to become involved with a grassroots advocacy group and read about the bills up for vote in the state legislature and US Congress.

◆ RESOURCES

National Conference of State Legislatures
1560 Broadway, Suite 700
Denver, CO 80202
Tel: 303-830-2200
Web: http://www.ncsl.org

Web Sites of the US House and Senate
http://www.house.gov
http://www.senate.gov

LOBBYISTS

✦ OVERVIEW

Lobbyists work to influence legislation on the federal, state, or local level on behalf of clients. Nonprofit organizations, labor unions, trade associations, corporations, and other groups and individuals use lobbyists to voice their concerns and opinions to government representatives. Lobbyists use their insights into legislative processes and their contacts in legislative offices to represent their clients' interests. Though most lobbyists are based in Washington, DC, many work elsewhere in the country representing client issues in city and state government. The growing use of the Internet is making a big impact on this field.

✦ EARNINGS

A lobbyist's income depends largely on the size of the organization represented. If you're a successful lobbyist working on behalf of large corporations, you can make well over $100,000 a year (with some bringing in more than $500,000). Beginning lobbyists, on the other hand, may make less than $20,000 a year as they build a client base.

According to a survey by the American Society of Association Executives published in 1997, directors of government relations of trade associations earned an annual average of $78,242.

✦ OUTLOOK

The number of special interest groups in the United States continues to grow, and as long as they continue to plead their causes before state and federal governments, lobbyists will be needed. However, because lobbying doesn't directly earn a profit for a business, the government relations department is often the first in a company to receive budget cuts. The American League of Lobbyists anticipates that the career will remain stable, though it's difficult to predict. In recent years, there has been a significant increase in registrations, but that is most likely a result of the Lobbying Disclosure Act of 1995 requiring registration.

✦ TRAINING

Almost all lobbyists have college degrees, and many have graduate degrees. Schools do not generally offer a specific curriculum that leads to a career as a lobbyist; your experience with legislation and policy-making is what will prove valuable to employers and clients. People typically take up lobbying after an earlier career—as a congressional staff member, for example. Degrees in law and political science are among the most beneficial for prospective lobbyists; others are journalism, public relations, and economics.

You won't need a license or certification to work as a lobbyist, but you will be required to register, either on the federal or state level.

A solid grasp of government and politics, a reputation as an honest and reliable person, an outgoing personality, and superior communication skills are some of the attributes of a good lobbyist.

 EXPLORING

Become an intern or volunteer in the office of a lobbyist, legislator, government official, special interest group, or nonprofit institution (especially one that relies on government grants). Working in these fields will introduce you to the lobbyist's world and provide early exposure to the workings of government.

Get involved in school government; writing for your school newspaper; and public relations, publicity, fund-raising, and advertising work for school and community organizations.

When major legislative issues are being hotly debated, write to your congressional representatives to express your views or even organize a letter-writing or telephone campaign; these actions are in themselves forms of lobbying.

 RESOURCES

American League of Lobbyists
PO Box 30005
Alexandria, VA 22310
Tel: 703-960-3011
Web: http://www.alldc.org

American Society of Association Executives
1575 I Street, NW
Washington DC, 20005
Tel: 202-626-2723
Web: http://www.asaenet.org

POLITICAL SCIENTISTS

◆ OVERVIEW

Political scientists study the structure and theory of government, usually as part of an academic faculty. They are constantly seeking both theoretical and practical solutions to political problems. They typically divide their responsibilities between teaching and researching. After compiling facts, statistics, and other research, they present their analyses in reports, lectures, and journal articles.

Political scientists who are not teachers work for labor unions, political organizations, political interest groups, business or industry, the government, or individual members of Congress.

◆ EARNINGS

Both the *Chronicle of Higher Education* and the American Association of University Professors conduct annual surveys of the salaries of college professors. In its 1998 survey, the *Chronicle* found that full professors at public universities received an average of $69,924 a year, while professors at private universities received $84,970 a year. Associate professors received an average of $50,186 annually at public universities and $56,517 at private. For assistant professors, the average salaries were $42,335 at public institutions and $47,387 at private institutions.

◆ OUTLOOK

In general, this field is expected to grow about as fast as the average for all occupations in the near future. The survival of political science departments depends on continued community and government support of education. The funding of humanities and social science programs is often threatened, resulting in budget cuts and hiring freezes. This makes for heavy competition for the few graduate assistantships and new faculty positions available. Also, there's not a great deal of mobility within the field; professors who achieve tenure generally stay in their positions until retirement.

◆ TRAINING

Some government jobs require only a bachelor's degree in political science, but you won't be able to pursue work in major academic institutions without a doctorate. Look for a school with a good internship program that can involve you with the US Congress or state legislature.

Because you'll be compiling information from a number of different sources, you must be well organized. You should also enjoy reading and possess a curiosity about world politics. People skills are important too, as you'll be working closely with students and other political scientists.

 EXPLORING

Write to college political science departments for information about their programs. You can learn a lot about the work of a political scientist by looking at college course lists and faculty bios. Many political science departments have Web pages with this information. You could also contact the office of your state's senator or congressional representative about applying to work as a page. These positions, which are highly competitive, give good insight into the inner workings of government.

 RESOURCE

American Political Science Association
1527 New Hampshire Avenue, NW
Washington, DC 20036
Tel: 202-483-2512
Web: http://www.apsanet.org

REGIONAL AND LOCAL OFFICIALS

◆ OVERVIEW

Regional and *local officials* hold positions in the legislative, executive, and judicial branches of government at the local level. They include mayors, commissioners, and city and county council members. These officials are elected to deal with issues such as public health, legal services, housing, and budget and fiscal management. They attend meetings, serve on committees, vote on laws, develop special programs, and generally work to meet the needs of their constituents and improve their communities.

◆ EARNINGS

In general, salaries for government officials tend to be lower than what the official could make working in the private sector. Many local officials volunteer their time or work part time. According to a salary survey published in 1998 by the International City/County Management Association (ICMA), the chief elected official of a city makes an average salary of $12,870 a year. City clerks, treasurers, and chief law enforcement officials fare better: Clerks earn about $37,000 a year; treasurers, $38,000; and chief law enforcement officials, $54,000.

The ICMA survey also compiled figures for county officials. A county's chief elected official averages $26,420 a year. County clerks make about $38,000; treasurers, $36,000; and chief law enforcement officials, $48,000.

◆ OUTLOOK

This field is expected to experience little change or grow more slowly than the average for all occupations in the near future. The form of your local government can be altered by popular vote, but these changes don't greatly affect the number of officials needed. Your chances of holding office will be greater in a smaller community. The races for part-time and nonpaying offices will also be less competitive.

Positions at the county level could be affected by the shift in costs from the federal government to states, which, in turn, may offer less aid to counties.

◆ TRAINING

To serve in local government, your experience and understanding of a city or county are generally more important than your educational background. But to serve as an executive or council member for a large city or county, you are likely to need an undergraduate degree. Recommended areas of study include public administration, law, economics, political science, history, and English.

To serve as a local official, you must have an intimate knowledge of and a personal commitment to your city and region. You should also be creative, good with people, and have strong communication and problem-solving skills.

 ## EXPLORING

Because governments are more accessible at the local level than at the state or federal level, it is easier for young people to get involved locally. Visit the county courthouse and volunteer in whatever capacity you can, or become involved with local elections. Many candidates welcome young people to assist with campaigns.

Another great way to learn about government is to get involved with an issue of interest to you. Maybe there's an old building in your neighborhood you'd like to save from destruction, or maybe you have some ideas for youth programs or programs for senior citizens. Research what's being done about your concerns and come up with solutions to offer local officials.

 ## RESOURCES

International City/County Management Association
777 North Capitol Street, NE, Suite 500
Washington, DC 20002-4201
Tel: 202-289-4262
Web: http://www.icma.org

National Association of Counties
440 First Street, NW
Washington, DC 20001
Tel: 202-393-6226
Web: http://www.naco.org

URBAN AND REGIONAL PLANNERS

✦ OVERVIEW

Urban and *regional planners,* often called *city planners,* work with local governments in the development and redevelopment of a city, metropolitan area, or region. They work to preserve historical buildings, protect the environment, and help manage a community's growth and change. Planners evaluate existing structures and help to integrate new buildings, houses, sites, and subdivisions into an overall city plan. Urban and regional planners who do not work for local government are employed in the private sector.

✦ EARNINGS

The median salary for all urban and regional planners is about $45,300, according to the American Planning Association's 1995 Salary Survey. Planners with less than five years of experience earned median salaries between $30,700 and $37,400; those with five to 10 years of experience, between $39,300 and $45,900; and those with more than 10 years of experience, between $52,100 and $63,300. Salaries for planning directors are considerably higher, ranging from $31,700 to $75,900 per year.

Consultants are generally paid on a fee basis. Their earnings are often high but vary greatly according to their reputation and work experience.

✦ OUTLOOK

The overall demand for city planners is expected to grow about as fast as the average through 2008, due in large part to shrinking government resources. Opportunities will exist for graduates with professional city and regional planning training, but the market is small and highly competitive. According to the *Occupational Outlook Handbook,* many job openings will result when experienced planners retire, change occupations, or leave the labor force for other reasons. Most new jobs will be in affluent and rapidly expanding communities.

✦ TRAINING

A college education—with a major in urban and regional planning, architecture, landscape architecture, civil engineering, or public administration—is the minimum requirement for trainee jobs with most municipal or other government boards and agencies. A master's degree in city or regional planning is usually needed as well.

To be a good city planner, you should have strong design and analytical skills, an understanding of spatial relationships, good imagination and vision, and keen problem-solving abilities.

 EXPLORING

Research the origins of your city by visiting the county courthouse and local library. Early photographs and maps of the city can give you an idea of what went into the planning of the area. Learn the histories of old buildings, and get involved in efforts to preserve buildings that are threatened.

You could also work with a teacher or academic advisor to arrange an interview with a planner. Another good way to gain insight into the field is to attend a meeting of a local planning commission, which, by law, is open to the public. Notices of meetings are usually published, but interested students can also call their local planning office for information.

✦ RESOURCES

American Planning Association
122 South Michigan Avenue, Suite 1600
Chicago, IL 60603
Tel: 312-786-6344
Web: http://www.planning.org

International City/County Management Association
777 North Capitol Street, NE, Suite 500
Washington, DC 20002-4201
Tel: 202-289-4262
Web: http://www.icma.org

*"Extracurricular activities are important because
they show that a student is involved and usually well-rounded.
Although extracurricular activities aren't
the first quality that we look for in an applicant,
they are especially important if the applicant is on the bubble
for a favorable admission decision."*

*– Mark Camper, Director of Admissions,
Liberty University, Lynchburg, Virginia*

CHAPTER 11

Theater and Drama

" *In general, I have always felt that individuals in extracurricular activities are better students, as the majority of the time it seems that they are more disciplined, more organized, and able to manage their time.* **"**

– Lena Throlson, Admissions Counselor,
Minot State University, Bottineau, North Dakota

✦ INTRODUCTION

With the explosion in the growth of cable television, DVDs, and other media, it truly seems that "all the world's a stage." Of course, Shakespeare's famous words apply to the theater, but careers in the dramatic field are growing more varied with each passing year.

Every time you watch an actor in a television show or listen to a singer at a concert, you can be sure there are a great many people behind the scenes, making sure the production runs smoothly. There are camera operators, lighting and sound crews, costume designers, agents, and more.

Think about how your favorite activities apply to the careers in this chapter. Cinematography might interest you if you are a movie buff. Or if you enjoy entertaining people, the section on acting might appeal to you. This chapter could help you find the professional role you are meant to play.

ACTORS

OVERVIEW

Actors play parts or roles in dramatic productions on the stage, in motion pictures, and on television and radio. They portray characters through speech, gesture, song, and dance. Acting is often seen as a glamorous job. In reality, it is demanding, tiring work requiring long hours of preparation and a special talent.

Actors in the theater may perform the same part many times a week for weeks or even years. Actors in films spend several weeks or months at a time involved in a production, often on location in a different part of the world. Television actors involved in a series, such as a soap opera or a situation comedy, generally work in 13-week cycles.

While studying and perfecting their craft, many actors work as extras—the nonspeaking characters who appear in the background on screen or stage. A great deal of an actor's time is spent in training and attending auditions.

EARNINGS

The average annual earnings for all motion picture actors are usually low for all but the best-known performers. The wage scale for actors is largely controlled through bargaining agreements reached by various unions in negotiations with producers. These agreements normally control the minimum salaries, hours of work permitted per week, and other conditions of employment. In addition, each artist enters into a separate contract that may provide for a higher salary.

The 1997 minimum weekly salary for actors in Broadway productions was $1,040, according to the Actors' Equity Association. Minimum salaries for those performing in "off Broadway" productions and smaller theaters ranged from $375 to $625 a week. A steady income is not the norm for most stage actors; average annual earnings in the late 1990s were $14,000.

According to the Screen Actors Guild, actors appearing in motion pictures or television shows were paid a daily minimum of $559, or $1,942 a week, in 1997. Extras earned a minimum of $99 a day. Motion picture actors may also receive additional payments known as residuals—additional fees whenever their work is rerun, sold for TV exhibition, or put on videocassette. Residuals often exceed the actors' original salary and account for about one-third of all actors' income.

Well-known actors have higher salary rates. Top film stars make up to $20 million a picture.

The annual earnings of actors in television and movies are affected by frequent periods of unemployment. Most guild members earn less than $5,000 a year from acting jobs.

 ## OUTLOOK

Jobs in acting are expected to grow faster than the average through the year 2008. The growth of satellite and cable television in the past decade has created a demand for more actors. The rise of home video has also created new acting jobs, as more and more films are made strictly for the home video market. Jobs in theater, on the other hand, face pressure as production costs rise and non-profit and smaller theaters lose funding.

Despite the growth in opportunities, however, there are many more actors than there are roles, and this is likely to remain true for years to come. Many actors must supplement their income by working in other areas.

 ## TRAINING

There are no minimum educational requirements to become an actor. However, at least a high school diploma is recommended, and having a college degree will often give you an advantage. It is assumed that the actor who has completed a liberal arts program in theater or dramatic arts is more capable of understanding the wide variety of roles that are available. Graduate degrees are almost always required to teach dramatic arts.

Prospective actors should have not only a great talent for acting but also a great determination to succeed. They also must have a good speaking voice and strong memorization capacity. The ability to sing and dance is always helpful.

Performers on the Broadway stage must be members of the Actors' Equity Association before being cast. While union membership may not always be required, many actors find it advantageous to belong to a union that covers their particular field of performing arts.

 ## EXPLORING

The best way to explore this career is to participate in school or local theater productions. Even working on the props or lighting crew will provide insight into the field. Also, attend as many dramatic productions as possible and try to talk with people who work in theater.

◆ **RESOURCES**

Acting Workshop On-Line

Actors' Equity Association

165 West 46th Street

New York, NY 10036

Tel: 212-869-8530

Web: http://www.execpc.com/~blankda/acting2.html

American Federation of Television and Radio Artists—Screen Actors Guild

260 Madison Avenue

New York, NY 10016

Tel: 212-532-0800

National Association of Schools of Theater

11250 Roger Bacon Drive, Suite 21

Reston, VA 22090

Tel: 703-437-0700

Screen Actors Guild

5757 Wilshire Boulevard

Los Angeles, CA 90036-3600

Tel: 213-549-6400

BROADCAST ENGINEERS

 OVERVIEW

Broadcast engineers, sometimes referred to as *broadcast technicians* or *broadcast operators,* operate and maintain the electronic equipment used to record and transmit radio and television programs. This equipment includes audio recorders, microphones, television cameras, lighting and sound devices, transmitters, and antennas. During a broadcast, engineers sit in a control room, working to ensure proper sound quality and smooth transitions between different video feeds, among other things. Broadcast engineers may work at a radio or television studio or from a satellite site.

 EARNINGS

Large stations usually pay higher wages than small stations, and television stations tend to pay more than radio stations. According to the 1996 National Association of Broadcasters survey, the salary for a radio station technician averaged $30,251 a year (this includes those with considerable experience; the lowest reported salary was $12,000). The salary for chief engineers averaged $46,602 a year. In television stations in 1995, an engineer's salary averaged $32,533 a year and a chief engineer's, $53,655 a year.

◆ **OUTLOOK**

According to the US Bureau of Labor Statistics, the overall employment of broadcast technicians is expected to grow about as fast as the average through the year 2008. Growth in the number of stations and number of programming hours should increase demand. A number of openings are expected to result from engineers leaving the broadcasting industry for other jobs in electronics. However, new technologies like computer programming and remote control transmitters may eliminate some of the traditional positions.

◆ **TRAINING**

To obtain an entry-level position in this field, you will need a high school diploma and technical school training. Positions that are more advanced require a bachelor's degree in broadcast communications or a related field. To become a chief engineer, you should aim for a bachelor's degree in electronics or electrical engineering. Because field technicians also act as announcers on occasion, speech courses and experience as an announcer for a school radio station can be helpful.

FCC licenses and permits are no longer required of broadcast engineers. However, certification from the Society of Broadcast Engineers is desirable.

Broadcast engineers must have an aptitude for working with highly technical electronic and computer equipment and strong attention to detail. They should enjoy both the technical and artistic aspects of the field and be able to communicate with a wide range of people.

✦ EXPLORING

Volunteering at a local radio or television station will provide good insight into the field of broadcast engineering. Most colleges and universities have radio and television stations where students can gain experience with broadcasting equipment. Many schools have clubs for persons interested in broadcasting. Such clubs often sponsor trips to broadcasting facilities and lectures by people working in the field. Local television station technicians can also be a good source of information. Exposure to broadcasting technology also may be obtained through building and operating an amateur (or ham) radio and experimenting with electronic kits.

✦ RESOURCES

Broadcast Education Association
1771 N Street, NW
Washington, DC 20036-2891
Tel: 202-429-5354
Web: http://www.beaweb.org

National Association of Broadcast Employees and Technicians
501 3rd Street, NW, 8th Floor
Washington, DC 20001
Tel: 202-434-1254
Web: http://union.nabetcwa.org/nabet/

Society of Broadcast Engineers
8445 Keystone Crossing, Suite 140
Indianapolis, IN 46240-2454
Tel: 317-253-1640
Web: http://www.sbe.org

CAMERA OPERATORS

 OVERVIEW

Camera operators use motion picture cameras, video cameras, and other equipment to photograph subjects or material for television programs, commercials, movies, film documentaries, and special events. They use different lighting, films, lenses, and filters to achieve the effect they want. They are often supported by an assistant or team of assistants. On productions they are not overseeing themselves, their direction typically comes from cinematographers or directors of photography.

 EARNINGS

Camera operators working on a motion picture typically get paid on a per-day basis. Their role in the creation of the movie may last several weeks or several months, but it is rare that a camera operator works 12 months out of the year. According to 1997 national wage estimates by the US Bureau of Labor Statistics, a camera operator for TV and motion pictures has a mean annual wage of $25,360. About 14 percent of the nation's camera operators make less than $12,000 a year, while 6 percent make over $50,000.

 OUTLOOK

The employment for motion picture camera operators will grow about as fast as the average for all other occupations, according to the US Department of Labor. The use of visual images continues to grow in areas such as communication, education, entertainment, marketing, and research and development. More businesses will make use of video training films and public relations projects that use film. The entertainment industries are also expanding. However, competition for positions is fierce.

◆ **TRAINING**

A college degree is not necessary to get a position as a camera operator, but a bachelor's degree in liberal arts or film studies provides a good background for work in the film industry. Still, practical experience and industry connections will provide the best opportunities for work. Upon completing an undergraduate program, you may wish to enroll in a master's or master's of fine arts program at a film school.

You must be able to work closely with others and respond quickly to instruction. In addition to the technical aspects of filmmaking, you should also understand its artistic nature.

EXPLORING

You can learn more about this field by joining a photography or camera club. Becoming involved with your school's media department may give you the opportunity to videotape sports events, concerts, or school plays. Some school districts have television stations where students can learn the basics of camera operation. A summer or part-time job in a camera shop will give you a basic understanding of photographic equipment.

RESOURCES

American Society of Cinematographers
1782 North Orange Drive
Hollywood, CA 90028
Tel: 323-969-4333
Web: http://www.cinematographer.com

International Alliance of Theatrical Stage Employees
1515 Broadway, Suite 601
New York, NY 10036
Tel: 212-730-1770
Web: http://www.iatse.lm.com

Society of Motion Picture and Television Engineers
595 West Hartsdale Avenue
White Plains, NY 10607
Tel: 914-761-1100
Web: http://www.smpte.org

CINEMATOGRAPHERS

 ## OVERVIEW

Cinematographers, also called *directors of photography,* are instrumental in establishing the mood of a film by putting the narrative aspects of a script into visual form. Cinematographers are responsible for the artistic elements of every shot, including framing, lighting, color level, and exposure. Cinematographers direct the camera crew and work closely with directors, deciding how to film each scene.

 ## EARNINGS

When starting out, apprentice filmmakers may make nothing; they may even be spending their own money to finance their projects. On the other end of the scale, well-established cinematographers working on big-budget productions can make well over a million dollars a year. The International Alliance of Theatrical Stage Employees establishes minimum wage scales for cinematographers who are union members, based on the nature of a film shoot. For feature film studio shoots, a cinematographer is paid $523 a day. For location shoots, the wage is $671 a day.

OUTLOOK

Because of fierce competition and a prediction of slow growth, it will be difficult to find employment in the film industry. However, the industry does thrive on new talent and original perspectives—with the right connections and samples of your filmmaking abilities, you may be able to find some opportunities. Outside of the film industry, you may find work with a video production company, advertising agency, or broadcasting company. Technical skills will be in high demand; cinematographers of the future will be working more closely with special effects houses, and digital technology will be prevalent.

TRAINING

A bachelor's degree in liberal arts or film studies provides a good background for work in the film industry, but practical experience and industry connections will provide the best job opportunities. Upon completing an undergraduate program, you may wish to enroll in a master's or master's of fine arts program at a film school.

Cinematographers must have the ability to keep abreast of technological innovations while maintaining an interest in the artistic and literary aspects of the profession. They must also be good leaders, able to choose and direct a crew effectively.

◆ EXPLORING

If you are interested in becoming a cinematographer, watch as many films as you can and study them closely for their different styles and effects. You can also experiment with composition and lighting if you have access to a camera or camcorder. Check with your school's media center or journalism department about shooting school events. Your school's drama club can involve you with writing and staging your own productions.

◆ RESOURCES

American Film Institute

2021 North Western Avenue
Los Angeles, CA 90027
Tel: 323-856-7600
Web: http://www.afionline.org

American Society of Cinematographers

1782 North Orange Drive
Hollywood, CA 90028
Tel: 323-969-4333
Web: http://www.cinematographer.com

COSTUME DESIGNERS

 OVERVIEW

Costume designers plan and create clothing and accessories for characters in a stage, film, television, dance, or opera production. They also work for figure skaters, circus performers, and rock groups, among others. They strive to capture the director's creative interpretation, the characters' personalities, and the period and style. Sketches are presented and approved, contract work is bid out, and actors measured and fitted. Costume designers work closely with drapers and sewers in costume shops, hair stylists, and makeup artists. They supervise fittings and attend all dress rehearsals to make final adjustments and repairs.

EARNINGS

Costume designers who work on Broadway or for dance companies in New York City must be members of United Scenic Artists union, which sets minimum fees. An assistant on a Broadway show earns about $775. A costume designer for a Broadway musical with a minimum of 36 actors earns around $17,500. For opera and dance companies, salary is usually by costume count. For feature films and television, costume designers earn daily rates for an eight-hour day or a weekly rate for an unlimited number of hours. Designers sometimes earn royalties on their designs.

Freelance costume designers might charge $90 to $500 per costume, but some costumes, such as those for figure skaters, can cost thousands of dollars. Freelancers often receive a flat rate for designing costumes for a show. For small and regional theaters, this rate may be in the $400 to $500 range; the flat rate for medium and large productions generally starts at around $1,000.

OUTLOOK

Theater budgets and support for the arts in general have come under pressure in recent years and have limited employment prospects for costume designers. Many theaters, especially small and nonprofit theaters, are cutting their budgets or doing smaller shows that require fewer costumes. The cable television business, however, is growing rapidly and will continue to grow in the next decade. As more cable television networks create original programming, demand for costume design in this area is likely to increase.

Competition is stiff and is expected to remain so throughout the next decade. The number of qualified costume designers far exceeds the number of jobs available, particularly in smaller cities.

◆ TRAINING

A college degree is not a requirement, but in this highly competitive field, it gives a sizable advantage, and most costume designers today have a bachelor's degree. Many art schools have BFA and MFA programs in costume design. A liberal arts school that has a strong theater program is also a good choice.

Costume designers need sewing, draping, and flat patterning skills, as well as training in basic design techniques and figure drawing.

Some theatrical organizations require membership in the United Scenic Artists union. Beginning designers become members by passing an exam. More experienced designers must submit a portfolio for review.

◆ EXPLORING

Those interested in a costume design career should join a theater organization, such as a school drama club or a community theater. School dance troupes and film classes also may offer opportunities to explore costume design.

Prospective costume designers can practice designing on their own, drawing sketches in a sketchbook and copying designs they see on television, in films, or on stage. They can also practice making costumes for themselves, friends, family members, and even dolls.

◆ RESOURCES

Costume Designers Guild
13949 Ventura Boulevard, Suite 309
Sherman Oaks, CA 91423
Tel: 818-905-1557

The Costume Society of America
55 Edgewater Drive
PO Box 73
Earleville, MD 21919-0073
Tel: 410-275-2329
Web: http://www.costumesocietyamerica.com

United States Institute of Theater Technology
6443 Ridings Road
Syracuse, New York 13206
Tel: 315-463-6463
Web: http://www.usitt.org

CREATIVE ARTS THERAPISTS

✦ OVERVIEW

Creative arts therapists treat and rehabilitate people with mental, physical, and emotional disabilities. They use the creative processes of music, art, dance/movement, drama, psychodrama, and poetry in their therapy sessions to determine the underlying causes of problems and help patients achieve their goals. For example, victims of domestic abuse, who might be reluctant or unable to talk about their situation, can be encouraged to express their feelings and anxieties through painting or sculpting. Creative arts therapists usually specialize in one type of therapeutic activity. Throughout the process, they regularly consult with other health care workers.

✦ EARNINGS

As noted in the *Occupational Outlook Handbook,* an American Therapeutic Recreation Association survey indicates that recreational therapists (who have many of the same duties and qualifications as creative arts therapists) earned about $27,760 in 1998. Those in consulting, supervisory, administrative, and teaching positions in the field earn around $42,000. Those working in government positions earned about $39,400 in 1997. Therapists just starting out in the field generally earn considerably less—usually between $20,000 and $26,000 per year.

Professional therapists who use arts therapy in conjunction with other specialties, such as psychiatry and psychology, may earn considerably more. Psychologists earned between $19,500 and $62,120 in 1997; creative arts therapists who complete their education in psychology can expect a salary in that range.

✦ OUTLOOK

The creative arts therapy professions are growing rapidly, and many new positions are created each year. Although enrollment in college therapy programs is increasing, new graduates are usually able to find at least part-time work. Job openings in nursing homes should continue to increase as the elderly population expands over the next few decades. Advances in medical technology and the recent practice of early discharge from hospitals should also create new opportunities in managed care facilities, chronic pain clinics, and cancer care facilities.

✦ TRAINING

To become a creative arts therapist, you typically need at least a bachelor's degree, usually in the area in which you wish to specialize. Most creative arts therapists must be certified by the nationally recognized association specific to their field. This often requires a graduate degree from a university with an accredited program. For instance, the American Association for Art Therapy requires a master's degree for accreditation. Many registered creative arts therapists also receive additional licenses as social workers, educators, mental health professionals, or marriage and family therapists.

Creative arts therapists should have a strong desire to help others and be able to work well with people of all backgrounds. They also should have patience, stamina, compassion, and a good sense of humor.

◆ EXPLORING

There are many ways to explore the career of creative arts therapist. You can talk with people working in the field and arrange to observe a creative arts therapy session. To see if you would be happy working in the field, try to arrange a part-time, summer, or volunteer position at a hospital, clinic, or nursing home. A summer job as an aide at a camp for disabled children would also provide insight into the nature of creative arts therapy, including both its rewards and demands.

◆ RESOURCES

American Art Therapy Association
1202 Allanson Road
Mundelein, IL 60060-3808
Tel: 847-949-6064
Web: http://www.arttherapy.org

American Music Therapy Association
8455 Colesville Road, Suite 1000
Silver Spring, MD 20910
Tel: 301-589-3300
Web: http://www.musictherapy.org/

National Coalition of Arts Therapies Associations
2117 L Street, NW, #274
Washington, DC 20037
Tel: 202-678-6787
Web: http://www.ncata.com/

DANCERS AND CHOREOGRAPHERS

✦ OVERVIEW

Dancers attempt to tell a story, interpret an idea, or simply express rhythm and sound by applying physical movements to music. Dancers typically perform in groups, but some appear in solo performances. Dance is often incorporated into other performances like operas and musicals, movies, and music videos. Styles include ballet, modern dance, and tap dance.

Choreographers create dances and dance routines and teach them to performers. Their dances may be original or an interpretation of a traditional work. Some dancers are also choreographers.

✦ EARNINGS

The minimum conditions of employment, hours of work, and salaries for a performing dancer are established between the unions and the producers. The minimum salary for dancers in ballet and other stage productions ranged from $610 to over $1,275 per week in the late 1990s, although many dance contracts are not for a whole year. Modern dance companies generally pay between $500 and $1,200 per week. Smaller companies might pay $50 per performance.

Dancers on television average $569 for a one-hour show (including rehearsal time); on cruise ships, between $200 and $500 per week plus room and board; in opera and stage performances, about $75 per performance with extra pay while touring; and on Broadway, a minimum of $700 per week.

Earnings for choreographers vary immensely. Earnings from performance royalties and fees range from nearly $1,000 a week in small professional theaters to over $30,000 for a Broadway production that requires up to 10 weeks of rehearsal time. For big-budget motion pictures, choreographers can earn an average of $3,000 a week, while those who work in television can earn up to $10,000 for a 14-day work period.

✦ OUTLOOK

Employment of dancers is expected to increase about as fast as the national occupational average through the next decade. Because dancers have relatively short careers, the turnover rate tends to be high, which bodes well for newcomers. However, the field can also be highly competitive and uncertain.

Television has provided additional positions, but the number of stage and screen productions is declining. The best opportunities may exist in regional ballet companies, opera companies, and dance groups affiliated with colleges and universities. The dancer who can move from performing to teaching will find employment possibilities in colleges, universities, and schools of dance; with civic and community groups; and at dance studios.

TRAINING

There are no formal educational requirements, but an early start and years of practice are basic to a successful career. A number of avenues for advanced training are also available. Some colleges and universities offer programs leading to a bachelor's or higher degree in dance. Another option is studying with professional dance teachers or attending a professional dance school.

Experience as a performer is usually required for teaching in professional schools, and graduate degrees are generally required by colleges and conservatories. Most dancers continue with classes in dance throughout their professional careers.

A dancer must be in excellent physical shape, have a feeling for music, a sense of rhythm, and grace and agility. Persistence and sensitivity are also important personal characteristics.

EXPLORING

Dancing is a highly competitive profession, and interested students should get as much experience as they can—as early as possible. It is wise to pursue every opportunity you can to perform publicly, in your community and elsewhere.

◆ RESOURCES

American Dance Guild
31 West 21st Street, 3rd Floor
New York, NY 10010
Tel: 212-627-3790

Dance USA
1156 15th Street, NW, Suite 820
Washington, DC 20005-1704
Tel: 202-833-1717
Web: http://www.danceusa.org

National Dance Association
1900 Association Drive
Reston, VA 22091
Tel: 800-321-0789
Web: http://www.aahperd.org/nda/nda-main.html

FILM AND TELEVISION DIRECTORS

◆ OVERVIEW

"Lights! Camera! Action!" aptly summarizes the major responsibilities of *film* and *television directors.* The director is an artist who coordinates the elements that shape a film or television production and is responsible for its overall style and quality.

Directors are well known for their part in guiding actors, but they are involved in much more, including casting, costuming, cinematography, editing, and sound recording. Directors must have insight into the many tasks that go into the creation of a film, and they must have a broad vision of how each part will contribute to the big picture.

◆ EARNINGS

Directors' salaries vary greatly. Most Hollywood film directors are members of the Directors Guild of America, and their union-negotiated contracts generally provide for minimum weekly salaries and are contingent on the cost of the picture being produced: for film budgets over $1.5 million, the weekly salary is about $8,000; for budgets of $500,000 to $1.5 million, it is $5,800 per week; and for budgets under $500,000, it is $5,100. Many directors negotiate extra conditions as well.

The average annual salary for a director of a television news program is about $50,000. A director at a small-market station may average as little as $28,000 per year, while a director employed by a larger network affiliate may make up to $120,000.

◆ OUTLOOK

According to the US Department of Labor, employment for motion picture and television directors is expected to grow faster than the average for all occupations through the year 2008. This optimistic forecast is based on the increasing global demand for films and television programming made in the United States as well as continuing US demand for home video rentals. However, most directors work on a freelance basis and competition is extreme.

Television offers directors a wider variety of employment opportunities. Cable television networks are proliferating, and directors are needed to help create original programming to fill this void.

TRAINING

There is no official educational requirement for a career as a director, but a high school diploma, at the very least, is recommended. Courses in English, art, theater, and history will give you a good foundation. A degree from a film school will certainly make you more marketable. There are more than 500 film studies programs offered by schools of higher education throughout the United States. However, competition is so pervasive in this industry that even film school graduates often find jobs scarce.

Today's motion picture director must have a high level of inspiration, creativity, and dedication. As is true of most artists, you will also need to have rich and varied experiences in order to create works that are intelligently crafted and speak to people of many different backgrounds.

EXPLORING

One way to explore this career is to be active in school and community drama productions, whether as performer, set designer, cue-card holder, or technical crew member. Many summer camps and workshops offer programs for high school students interested in film work. In high school and beyond, pay attention to motion pictures—watch them at every opportunity, both at the theater and at home. Study your favorite television shows to see what makes them interesting.

◆ RESOURCES

American Film Institute
2021 North Western Avenue
Los Angeles, CA 90027
Tel: 323-856-7600
Web: http://www.afionline.org

Broadcast Education Association
1771 N Street, NW
Washington, DC 20036-2891
Tel: 202-429-5354
Web: http://www.beaweb.org

Directors Guild-Assistant Directors Training Program
15260 Ventura Boulevard, Suite 1200-A
Sherman Oaks, CA 91403
Tel: 818-382-1744
Web: http://www.dga.org

FILM EDITORS

◆ OVERVIEW

Film editors perform an essential role in the motion picture and television industries—they take unedited film or videotape and use specialized equipment to improve it and prepare it for viewing. So that they have a good feel for the purpose and scope of the project, film editors work closely with producers and directors throughout the entire production process. They are usually the final decision-makers when it comes to choosing which segments will stay in the film, which segments will be cut, and which need to be redone. They look at the quality of each film segment, its dramatic value, and its relationship to other segments, and then they arrange the segments in a sequence that creates the most effective finished product.

◆ EARNINGS

Film editors are not as highly paid as others working in the film or television industries. According to 1997 national wage estimates of the US Bureau of Labor Statistics, the mean annual wage for film editors was $40,740. A small percentage of film editors earn less than $18,000 a year, while some earn over $90,000. The most experienced and sought after film editors can command much higher salaries. The Avid Film Camp advises students that they may make as little as $15,000 a year in this career but notes that there are some editors at the top of the field who make over $900,000 a year.

◆ OUTLOOK

The outlook for film editors is good. The growth of cable television and an increase in the number of independent film studios will translate into greater demand for film editors. This will also force the largest studios to offer more competitive salaries in order to attract the best film editors.

The digital revolution will greatly affect film editing. Editors will work much more closely with special effects houses in putting together films. This technology may allow prospective film editors more direct routes into the industry, but the majority will have to follow traditional routes, obtaining years of hands-on experience.

◆ TRAINING

On-the-job experience is the best guarantee for lasting employment in this field, but some studios require their film editors to have a bachelor's degree.

Recommended degrees include English, journalism, theater, and film, with courses in cinematography and audiovisual techniques. Universities with departments of broadcast journalism offer courses in film editing and also may have contacts at local television stations. Some two-year colleges also offer film editing courses.

Training as a film editor takes from four to 10 years. Many film editors learn much of their work on the job as an assistant.

Film editors must be able to work cooperatively with other creative people, maintain confidence in the presence of other professionals, and have an understanding of the history of film and the narrative form in general. Computer skills are also important.

✦ EXPLORING

Many high schools have film clubs and/or offer film classes. Some have cable television stations affiliated with the school district, which might give students the opportunity to create and edit short programs. Large television stations and film companies occasionally seek volunteers or student interns. Most people in the film industry start out doing minor production tasks. By working closely with a film editor, a production assistant can learn television or film operations as well as film editing techniques. The best way to prepare for a career as a film editor is to read widely and watch films, paying close attention to how the story and scenes are presented.

✦ RESOURCES

American Cinema Editors
1041 North Formosa Avenue
West Hollywood, CA 90046
Tel: 213-850-2900
Web: http://www.ace-filmeditors.org

American Film Institute
2021 North Western Avenue
Los Angeles, CA 90027
Tel: 323-856-7600
Web: http://www.afionline.org

LIGHTING TECHNICIANS

 OVERVIEW

Lighting technicians set up and control lighting equipment for live and recorded television broadcasts, motion pictures, and video productions. They begin by consulting with the production director and technical director to determine the types of lighting and special effects needed and when changes should take place. During filming, lighting technicians follow a script or instructions from a technical director and adjust the lighting accordingly. They use spotlights and floodlights, mercury-vapor lamps, white and colored lights, reflectors, and a large array of dimming, masking, and switching controls.

EARNINGS

Salaries for lighting technicians vary according to experience level. Annual income is also determined by the number of projects a technician is hired for—the most experienced technicians can work year-round on a variety of projects, while those starting out may go weeks without work. Union daily minimum pay for gaffers (chief lighting technicians) and best boys (gaffers' assistants) is between $230 and $250. Experienced technicians can negotiate for much higher wages.

OUTLOOK

As long as the movie and television industries continue to grow, opportunities will be available for lighting technicians. With the expansion of the cable market, lighting technicians may find work in more than one area.

The increasing use of visual effects and computer generated imagery will likely have an impact on the work of lighting technicians; through computer programs, filmmakers and editors can adjust lighting themselves. However, live-action shots are still integral to the filmmaking process, and getting these shots requires trained lighting technicians.

 TRAINING

There is strong competition for broadcast and motion picture technician positions, and, in general, only well-prepared technicians get good jobs. You should attend a two-year postsecondary training program in electronics and broadcast technology, especially if you hope to advance to a supervisory position. Film schools also offer useful degrees in production, as do theater programs. For a position as a chief engineer, a bachelor's degree is usually required.

To succeed in this field, you should have good communication skills and be a dependable team player. The work also requires good physical strength and an inclination toward working with electronics.

EXPLORING

Prospective lighting technicians should learn as much as possible about electronics. Valuable learning experiences include handling the lighting for a school stage production, building a radio from a kit, and working in an appliance or TV repair shop. High school shop or vocational teachers may be able to arrange a presentation by a qualified lighting technician.

You can also learn a lot about the technical side of production by operating a camera for your school's journalism or media department. Try videotaping a play, concert, or sporting event for insight into production work. You may also have the opportunity to intern or volunteer with a local technical crew for a film or TV production. Check the Internet or your state's film commission for production schedules.

RESOURCES

American Film Institute
2021 North Western Avenue
Los Angeles, CA 90027
Tel: 323-856-7600
Web: http://www.afionline.org

American Society of Cinematographers
1782 North Orange Drive
Hollywood, CA 90028
Tel: 323-969-4333
Web: http://www.cinematographer.com

MAKEUP ARTISTS

OVERVIEW

Makeup artists prepare actors for performances on stage and before cameras. They apply foundations and powders to keep actors looking natural under the harsh lighting of stage and film productions. They accent or downplay an actor's natural features and conceal scars, skin blemishes, and wrinkles—or apply these features when needed for the character. Makeup artists read the script and meet with the director and technicians to determine the age of the characters, the setting and time period, lighting effects, and other details. They style and color hair and apply wigs, bald caps, beards, and sideburns. Makeup artists are also in charge of maintaining actors' makeup throughout filming.

Many makeup artists work as freelancers, contracting work from studios, theaters, production companies, and special effects houses.

EARNINGS

Makeup artists usually contract with a production, negotiating a daily rate. An experienced makeup artist can make around $300 a day on a film with a sizable budget; some of the top makeup artists in the business command around $1,000 a day. Theatrical makeup artists can make comparable daily wages on Broadway or in a theater in a large city. Small theaters, on the other hand, may pay only around $50 a day. As an independent contractor, you won't be making a steady yearly salary. You may work long hours for several weeks and then go without work for several weeks.

OUTLOOK

Makeup artists will find increased opportunities in the film and television industries in the near future. The original programming needed to fill the schedules of new cable channels should result in more jobs for makeup artists. Makeup effects artists will find challenging and well-paying work as the film industry pushes the envelope on special effects. These makeup artists will likely use computers more and more, as digital design becomes an important tool in creating film effects.

Due to lack of funding, many theaters will be unable to hire the cast and crew needed for productions. There has been a revived interest in Broadway, however, which could result in better opportunities in traveling productions, as well as regional theaters across the country.

TRAINING

Because of the freelance nature of this business, experience is generally more valuable than education. You can enter the business right out of high school, but you must be very ambitious, enthusiastic, and capable of seeking out successful mentors. This can mean a lot of time working for free or for very little pay. A good college or professional program can open doors for you and get you your first jobs. Among the most highly respected schools for makeup artists in film are the Joe Blasco Schools of Hollywood and Florida. Some people in the business have cosmetology degrees, but most have received bachelor's degrees or master's degrees in theater, art history, film history, photography, or fashion merchandising.

Patience and the ability to get along well with people are important for a makeup artist, as is attention to detail, persistence, and the ability to work well under pressure.

EXPLORING

Your high school drama department or a community theater can provide you with great experience in hair and makeup and the chance to see your work under stage lights. A high school video production team or film department may also offer opportunities for makeup experience.

Volunteering with your state's film commission can give you a lot of insight into the film production process. Also, many universities and colleges now have film departments; you could either take film courses or volunteer to assist with the production of a student film.

◆ RESOURCES

Make-up Artist Magazine
PO Box 4316
Sunland, CA 91041
Tel: 818-504-6770
Web: http://www.makeupmag.com

Theater Communications Group
355 Lexington Avenue
New York, NY 10017
Tel: 212-697-5230

PRODUCTION ASSISTANTS

✦ OVERVIEW

Production assistants perform a variety of tasks for a television or film producer and other staff members, ensuring that daily operations run as smoothly as possible. Some production assistants perform substantive jobs, such as reviewing scripts; others primarily run errands. Duties might include photocopying scripts for actors, assisting in setting up equipment, keeping the producer's folder of production details up to date, and keeping files in order, including contracts, budgets, script changes, and other records. Production assistants work hard and often keep long hours.

EARNINGS

Because working as a production assistant is the starting point for most professionals and artists in the film industry, many people volunteer their time at first. Assistants who can negotiate payment may make between $200 and $400 a week, but they may work on only a few projects a year. Production assistants working full time in an office may start at around $20,000 a year but with experience can make around $65,000.

If working full time, you may belong to the Office and Professional Employees International Union which negotiates salaries. Experienced script supervisors, production office coordinators, and continuity coordinators can join Local #161 of the International Alliance of Theatrical Stage Employees. As a member, you may be entitled to over $180 a day when working for a production company.

OUTLOOK

There will always be a need for assistants in film and television production. However, since it is such a good entry-level position for someone who wants to make connections and learn about the industry, competition for jobs can be tough. The best opportunities are in Los Angeles and New York City—the production hubs of the industry.

✦ TRAINING

There are no formal education requirements for production assistants. You can learn much of what you'll need to know on the set of a film. Though a film school education can't guarantee entry into the business, it can give you an understanding of the industry and help you make connections. A listing of film schools is available from the American Film Institute. You may choose to major in English or theater as an undergraduate, then apply to graduate film schools.

As a production assistant, you'll need to have a love of the industry as well as an outgoing and agreeable personality, a willingness to follow instructions and perform simple tasks, the ability to learn quickly, strong organizational skills, and great ambition and dedication.

◆ EXPLORING

There are many ways to gain experience with filmmaking. Some high schools have film clubs and classes in film or video. Experience in theater can also be useful. To learn more, you can work as a volunteer for a local theater or a low-budget film project; these positions are often advertised in local trade publications. You may also be able to volunteer with your state's film commission.

◆ RESOURCES

American Film Institute
2021 North Western Avenue
Los Angeles, CA 90027
Tel: 323-856-7600
Web: http://www.afionline.org

American Society of Cinematographers
1782 North Orange Drive
Hollywood, CA 90028
Tel: 323-969-4333
Web: http://www.cinematographer.com

SPECIAL EFFECTS TECHNICIANS

 OVERVIEW

Special effects technicians work to make the illusion of movies, theater, and television seem real. When a director wants us to see a man turn into a wolf or a train explode in a fiery crash, it is the job of special effects technicians to make it happen. They work with a variety of materials and techniques to produce the fantastic visions and seemingly real illusions that add dimension to a film. The work of a special effects technician is highly creative; often the director has only a general idea of what he or she wants and the technicians must come up with the artistic and functional specifics. Specialized areas include mechanical effects, computer animation, make-up effects, and pyrotechnics.

 EARNINGS

The average daily pay for beginning special effects technicians is $100 to $200 per day, while more experienced technicians can earn $300 per day or more. A 1998 member salary survey conducted by the International Alliance of Theatrical Stage Employees and Moving Picture Machine Operators of the United States and Canada found that character animators, CGI effects animators, and art directors had median yearly earnings of around $100,000. On the low end of the scale, these professionals earned around $55,000, and on the high end, $350,000. Effects assistants had beginning wages of around $45,000, and median wages of $60,000.

✦ **OUTLOOK**

The competition for jobs in film special effects houses is fierce. According to *Forbes* magazine, the film industry spent over $600 million in special effects in 1997—twice as much as in 1993. And while some special effects companies are very profitable, others are struggling to make enough money to meet their expenses. The cost of the effects, including salaries for top technicians, are increasing, while film producers decrease their special effects budgets.

Digital technology will continue to rapidly change the industry. Experts predict that within 10 years, film will be eliminated and movies will be shot and projected digitally, expanding the role of special effects technicians.

TRAINING

As a special effects technician, you'll rely on a mix of science and art. While there are no formal educational requirements for entry into this field, some universities have film and television programs that include courses in special effects. Special effects technicians also might major in theater, art history, or photography. In a masters of fine arts program, you can gain hands-on experience in theater production and filmmaking.

To work as a pyrotechnics specialist, you will need a license in most states in order to handle explosives and firearms.

Special effects work is physically and mentally demanding. Technicians must be able to work well with others, follow instructions carefully and quickly, endure long hours, and work in sometimes physically uncomfortable situations.

EXPLORING

Students who like to build things and tend to be curious about how things work might be well suited to a career in special effects. To learn more about the profession, you might work on a high-school drama production as a stage hand, "techie," or make-up artist. Community theaters and independent filmmakers may offer volunteer opportunities. If computer animation interests you, gain as much computer experience as you can.

◆ RESOURCES

American Film Institute
2021 North Western Avenue
Los Angeles, CA 90027
Tel: 323-856-7600
Web: http://www.afionline.org

Animation World Network
6525 Sunset Boulevard, Garden Suite 10
Hollywood, CA 90028
Tel: 323-468-2554
Web: http://www.awn.com

The Visual Effects Society
15118 Valley Vista Boulevard
Sherman Oaks, CA 91403
Tel: 818-789-7083
Web: http://www.visual-effects-society.org

Resources

BOOKS

Bartlett, John. *The Future Is Ours: A Handbook for Student Activists in the 21st Century.* New York: Henry Holt and Company, 1996

Bellingrath, George C. *Qualities Associated With Leadership in the Extra-Curricular Activities of the High School.* New York: AMS Press

Duper, Linda Leeb. *160 Ways to Help the World: Community Service Projects for Young People.* New York: Checkmark Books, 1996

Joekel, Richard. *A Handbook for the Student Activity Adviser.* National Association of Student Councils, 1979

Klesse, Edward. *Student Activities: The Third Curriculum.* Reston, VA: National Association of Secondary School Principals, 1994

Kurtz, Jan. *The ABCs of Advising Student Activities.* Reston, VA: National Association of Secondary School Principals, 1987

Laird, Joanne. *Survival Guide for Class and Club Advisers.* Reston, VA: National Association of Secondary School Principals, 1995

✦ Osborn, Patricia. *School Newspaper Adviser's Survival Guide.* New York: Center for Applied Research in Education, 1997

Student Council Handbook. Reston, VA: National Association of Secondary School Principals, 1999

Willingham, Warren. *Success in College: The Role of Personal Qualities and Academics.* New York: The College Board, 1985

ASSOCIATIONS

National Association of Secondary School Principals
Department of Student Activities
1904 Association Drive
Reston, VA 20191-1537
Tel: 703-860-0200
Web: http:///www.nassp.org/

"Serves education leaders in middle level schools and high schools, including administrators, teachers, students, and others interested in education and the welfare of today's youth." NASSP is the parent organization of the National Honor Society, National Association of Student Councils, National Association of Student Activity Advisers, and Middle Level Student Activities Association. The Association offers a variety of publications for advisers and students who are interested in co-curricular activities.

Future Business Leaders of America Phi Beta Lambda
1912 Association Drive
Reston, VA 20191-1591
Tel: 800-325-2946
Email: general@fbla.org
Web: http://www.fbla-pbl.org/

A "nonprofit educational association of students preparing for careers in business and business-related fields." The association offers the following newsletters for students: *Tomorrow's Business Leader* and *PBL Business Leader.*

◆ Health Occupations Students of America
6021 Morriss Road, Suite 111
Flower Mound, TX 75028
Tel: 800-321-HOSA
Email: info@hosa.org
Web: http://www.hosa.org/

A national vocational student organization that promotes career opportunities in the health care industry.

Index